The Essence of
Religions

The Essence of Religions

A Glimpse of Heaven
in the Near-Death Experience

CHRISTOPHOR COPPES

SelectBooks, Inc.
New York

This edition published by SelectBooks, Inc.
For information address SelectBooks, Inc., New York, New York.

First Edition

ISBN 978-1-59079-245-2

Cataloging-in-Publication Data
Coppes, Christophor.
  The essence of religions : a glimpse of heaven in the near-death experience / Christophor Coppes.
        p. cm.
  Includes bibliographical references.
  Summary: "Author compares essences of the five mainstream religions to revelations during near-death experiences when people have a glimpse of heaven as our birthright. He argues that while near-death encounters encompass beliefs of world religions, people emerge with messages about greater universality, largely a feeling of our interconnectiveness with a being of comprehensive, unconditional compassion and love "--Provided by publisher.
  ISBN 978-1-59079-245-2 (pbk. : alk. paper)
  1. Near-death experiences--Religious aspects. 2. Future life. 3. Heaven. I. Title.
  BL535.C67 2012
  202'.3--dc23
                        2012013615

Interior book design by Janice Benight

Manufactured in the United States of America
10 9 8 7 6 5 4 3 2 1

Dedicated to The Light:

BRAHMAN, THE BUDDHAS, YHWH, GOD, ALLAH

A Review of *The Essence of Religions: A Glimpse of Heaven in the Near-Death Experience*

By Eben Alexander III, MD

The phenomenon of near-death experiences (NDEs) is relatively new, having originated in large measure because of the advent of medical techniques, over the last few decades, for resuscitating those who have suffered a cardiac arrest. Sporadic cases of those who had apparently "died" and then come back to life go back for millennia, but the vast majority of such cases have occurred in the last half-century. The initial professional view of these elaborate journeys as hallucinations or dreams has given way to a widespread scientific recognition that the similarities of these extraordinary recollections across a wide range of medical conditions, personal and cultural backgrounds, and prior belief systems (religious, scientific, etc.) suggest a common underlying reality as their basis. The consensus among those scientists who study them is that they are not simply "tricks of the dying brain," or brain-based phenomena at all. In fact, they often share similarities with the stories of religious mystics and prophets over millennia. I suspect that much of our religious literature elaborating on the spiritual realm originated in "near-death" and similar mind-states.

Christophor Coppes, chairman of the Dutch branch of the International Association for Near-Death Studies (IANDS), has provided a scholarly assessment of the similarities and differences found in the world's five major religions when compared with the prominent lessons learned from near-death experiences. Although the real essences of each of the five main religions can be found in NDEs, not all essences of NDEs can be found in each of the religions separately. He rightfully concludes that the NDE seems *more comprehensive* than each of the religions individually.

As we move away from worn-out dogma from both the religious and scientific realms toward a contemporary synthesis of understanding about our existence, Christophor's refreshing and comprehensive analysis of major religions in light of the profound lessons from numerous NDE journeyers offers a rich new tapestry of understanding that I find most valuable.

Eben Alexander III, MD
Lynchburg, Virginia, USA
January 28, 2013

Contents

PREFACE

This book is written to discourage any kind of misuse of religions. It is meant to provide the much-needed tools to reconsider some of the dogmas of the five major world religions that are detrimental to human beings and to the world at large. It is also meant to replace these detrimental dogmas with something more uplifting to greatly benefit us all. This can be described as a true alignment with the unconditional love that we call God, Allah, YHWH, Brahman, or the Buddhas, or The Light that appears in the visions of those who have had near-death experiences.

People who have had a near-death experience are convinced that they had a glimpse of heaven. Although each near-death experience is unique, we find recurring messages in them. I have become convinced that by acknowledging the wonderful messages from those who had these experiences, people can become happier. In addition, the messages relayed to them from The Light can make our world a better place. Therefore, it is interesting to compare the essences of the five religions with the essences of NDEs. I compare what people have related about these experiences, in which they reveal their profound beliefs about life and afterlife, with the essential spiritual beliefs about the meaning of life and afterlife in the five mainstream religions.

In the essences of each of these religion's spiritual beliefs there are some wonderful characteristics. I explain what these are and what their parallels are with NDEs. At the same time I explain where the religions go astray. My conclusion is that while the essences of the beliefs in these religions can be found in NDEs, not all essences of NDEs can be found in each of the religions. Consequently, the beliefs and spiritual insights of those who have had near-death experiences seem to be more universal than each of the religions individually.

I first discuss the essences of NDEs. The most important characteristic of this experience is the feeling that we are being surrounded by a comprehensive and unconditional love. This feeling is there for many who have been in this state of being, but they are convinced that in principle it is there for everyone. Essential is also the feeling that we are all profoundly interconnected, and that everyone is important; there are no lesser souls. And there is the insight that from the moment we are born we have the right to eventually return to the place of The Light. In other words, heaven is our birthright. The fact that some people have distressful NDEs is also discussed, and a resolution for this is explained within this context.

Next, the essences of the five mainstream religions of Hinduism, Buddhism, Judaism, Christianity, and Islam are evaluated. Many interesting parallels with NDEs are discovered, but there are also some remarkable differences. At the end of each chapter examining a specific religion there is a section called "foolish fixations," in which terrible excesses of that religion are discussed. These excesses demonstrate that in all religions one can find developments away from their core and from the most important thing there is: comprehensive and unconditional love. Religions are only good when they really bring people closer to God, Allah, JHWH, Brahman, or to enlightenment represented by the Buddhas. And religions start to be harmful when they are used by people to demean others, or when their content is adjusted by some to impose their will on others.

In the last chapter some of the most important topics of the near-death experience are summarized and compared with spiritual insights from the five religions. These topics involve the belief that God or The Light is indescribable, that God or The Light is in all of us, that love and compassion are the most important things there are in our existence, that each person has a task to fulfill in life, that there is free will, that everything in our life is recorded, and that there is no final judgment of us or a punishment for our earthly transgressions.

In this way, it is revealed to us that the more we are aligned with the unconditionally loving Light, the better our lives and the world will be.

A Partial View of the Elephant

The six blind men didn't agree. According to a folk story from India the first blind man, who was standing at the rear of an elephant, said that an elephant resembled a sturdy piece of rope with a little brush at the end. The second blind man disputed his view. He stood in front of this great animal and was convinced that an elephant was equal to a flexible thick hose. The third felt big flaps that moved and made a lot of wind. Therefore, he was sure it was a fan. The fourth, who got hold of a tusk, said that an elephant was pointy and hard, like a spear. The fifth blind man, who got on his knees, felt the elephant's legs as great pillars of trees. And the last man, who was standing at the elephant's side, was absolutely sure that the animal was simply a massive wall.

They all had the complete picture wrong, but for a small part of it each one was right. In my opinion this also applies to religions. For a small part everyone is right, but no one can tell us what the entirety really looks like.

Should they put aside their fixation to be proved right and instead work together, they would come closer to knowing the truth about our spiritual nature. For that, they would only have to look at the essences of each other's beliefs. The problem is that fervent adherents of a belief are not normally able to think beyond their limited perspective. Their narrow-mindedness obscures their view of the world. However, we don't have to be constrained by their limiting viewpoints. We can break free and compare the essences ourselves.

Although through a similar comparison of our different beliefs we would probably get closer to the truth, we have to realize that we will possibly never be able to fathom everything. In that respect our comparison with the blind men can be pursued. Even after a close collaboration with each other they will never know exactly what an elephant looks like. For example, they will never know how graciously an elephant moves, how much pleasure he gets when he sprays himself with dust or water, how limber he is with his trunk, or which color grey he is, or see how his beautiful orange-red eyes turn to keep an eye on them.

One way to get a bit closer to the truth about our spiritual nature is to hear what people who have had a Near-Death Experience (NDE) have to say. These people experience what happens in the first moments after their death, when they often visit a paradise-like world that doesn't resemble our earthly world at all. Their experiences show that we are able to leave our body and have an impression of where we will go when we die. The people who experience this perceive that life doesn't end with death, and that we will not be alone when we pass away. When entering that other world we seem to meet other beings or entities and are enveloped in some sort of wonderful, indescribably beautiful, and unconditionally loving Light, full of forgiveness.

During their NDE people have the sensation that they seem to find the answer to the question of what the purpose is for their stay on Earth. However, when they are pulled back from their NDE and arrive again in our four space-time dimensional world, they cannot clearly remember this well-defined purpose. In spite of this they remain convinced that everything on Earth has a good reason, even the sorrows and setbacks. Their near-death experiences seem to have contained a message about what we should and shouldn't do with our lives and how together we can make a wonderful world. The main message from the people who have experienced NDEs is that love, in general, is by far the most important aspect in this world. Increasing love and compassion is something they feel would be exactly in alignment with The Light that the near-death experiencers (NDEers) often meet during their experience. This Light is always described by them as a powerful, unconditional love. Another important message they want to give us is that we all are thoroughly interconnected with each other and with The Light.

These and other messages from those who have had an NDE come right into the domain of religions. Up until now all religions have said they have the answers to many, if not all, spiritual questions relating to the purpose of our life: the way we should lead it and what will happen to us when we die. By forcefully maintaining that point of view over a long period, religions claimed to have a monopoly on answers to spiritual questions. But NDEs show that the search for these answers is far from over.

For that quest it is of importance to make comparisons between NDEs and the content of the main world religions, and to do this we need to determine the essence of each of the religions. That is why in this book I will discuss the mainstream ideas of the five great religions: Hinduism, Buddhism, Judaism, Christianity and Islam. I will start with Hinduism because it is probably the oldest religion on Earth. Next, I will proceed with the religion that originated from it, Buddhism. Then I will go on to discuss Judaism, which is the oldest religion after Hinduism. Although Judaism is not a world religion in the sense that very many people follow it, it did lay the foundation for both Christianity and Islam, and these religions will be subsequently discussed.

I will show that the essence of each of these religions has some wonderful characteristics. You'll also see that their essence is always aimed at the best for humans and that in this way religions are very positive. More interesting is that the true essences in each religion coincide with what we can find in NDEs. There are astonishing parallels! However, for the other way around this doesn't hold. Not all essences of the NDEs can be found in each of the religions. This is an interesting conclusion because it seems to indicate that NDEs are more universal than each of the religions separately. Consequently, understanding the aspects of NDEs and the religions together can help us to come closer to the truth.

Therefore, each religion is worthwhile, and for our search for the truth it is good to acknowledge the essentials of each of them and their parallels to NDEs. For this reason I will conclude in the last chapter with a list of the essential elements of the five religions and their parallels I have observed with NDEs. It will be up to you to evaluate this and to continue your own search for spiritual truths.

This will not be an easy search since many differences among the religions are caused by the fact that they are at least partially man-made. For example, religions are not static; they change over the course of time. People regularly had to reinterpret the traditional beliefs to make them compatible with the ever-changing aspects of the world around them. A reinterpretation can lead to meaningful new principles, but also to foolish fixations that will only take people further away from the essential beliefs. Those foolish fixations can take different forms. Some can be amusing or maybe just inconvenient, but they can also be gruesome, as in some beliefs held by the Aztecs. At some point in time they came to believe that the sun would rise only when it had nourishment in the form of human blood. To ensure this, some Aztec tribes had a special ritual in which blood was produced by cutting out the heart from a living body.

While the five religious traditions are rarely this appalling, we can identify in each of them certain developments that made them turn away from their own essence and of the concept of unconditional love and forgiveness that we find as the foremost essence in NDEs. That is why after discussing each religion and its parallels to NDEs, I will also try to identify certain foolish religious fixations. I do that just to show that religions are at least partially man-made and that we should always ask ourselves whether we are trying to follow the essence of The Light.

~ 2 ~

Near-Death Experiences

UNCONDITIONAL LOVE & INTERCONNECTEDNESS

Extraordinary Experiences

NDEs are extraordinary. Many who have them are convinced that the remarkable event was their first step into their afterlife. They are absolutely sure that they have been in heaven, or at least on its doorstep. Often these experiences occur during a medically critical situation when the person is truly "near death," for instance after a serious accident or a cardiac arrest. But it is now acknowledged that NDEs can also occur in other situations when there is no life-threatening medical situation. There have been reports of very deep NDEs during deep meditation or during an existential crisis, and I have even heard from one NDEer who had his very deep NDE while sitting on the beach.[1]

NDEs are very special to those who have had them. They are ineffable and people have a hard time finding the right words to express what they have gone through. Nevertheless, people are convinced that what they felt and encountered during this time was "real." Often they say that their experience was more real than everyday life. Interestingly, all NDEs are quite different; no two NDEs are the same. Most times there is a description of a wonderful feeling of peace, quiet, and happiness. However, distressing NDEs have been reported often enough to rule out that they were statistical "outliers." These experiences can sometimes be extremely unpleasant or even hellish.

NDEs generally start with an out-of-body experience, during which they can see what is happening to their body that they are leaving behind. There may be a tunnel that they fly through at the speed of light. They may enter an unearthly environment, sometimes with cities or gardens, but always extremely beautiful with colors and scents that cannot be found on Earth. All knowledge seems freely available to tap into. Time and space seem not to pose any limitation. One even said that "time was there all at the same time."[2] Sometimes beings of light are encountered and occasionally people have met The Light, which is always an absolute and overpowering experience. Some NDEers said that in the presence of this Light they had a review of their life.

Even without an encounter with The Light or a life review, the experience is overwhelming. Consequently, NDEers will never be the same as before. People who have had an NDE have changed. Sometimes the alteration in their personalities and character may not seem very clear, and it may take many years to mature, but change there is. There is a wide range of after-effects. NDEers become more sensitive, more intuitive, and sometimes even have paranormal experiences. After the event they are often more sensitive to sounds, light, scent, and, interestingly, this often includes their reaction to medications. The normal dose of something can suddenly be too much for them. Importantly, their love for other people and nature increases; it becomes more a universal kind of love. They start having more respect for others, often becoming less judgmental and more tolerant. Their interest in money, social status, and power generally reduces or even vanishes all together. They lose fear of death because they thoroughly believe that they have seen the afterlife and know that consciousness doesn't end with the physical death. All of this is a good reason to compare NDEs with religions, but first we have to take a closer look at some of the aspects of NDEs.

The Light

Some see The Light. That indescribably beautiful Light. It is breathtaking. It is irresistible—like a sun, but many times more beautiful and more radiant. It is impossible for people to give a good description. They claim it is brilliant, it is bright white, it has all colors; and at the same time it has no color. It is like the most beautiful explosion of fireworks we have seen in our life. Nevertheless, it is soft—it does not hurt our eyes. It attracts us like a magnet. Moving into that Light is great. It is like coming home. It is our home. The Light is reassuring; it radiates unconditional love and an enormous forgiveness. The Light is pure love, pure peace, pure perfection. The love of The Light is many times stronger than the love someone feels for his or her children. The Light has an enormous knowledge; it knows everything. And at that time we seem to know everything, too.

The strength of The Light is described as being thousands of times more powerful than the bomb on Hiroshima. It is the most powerful entity that exists. It has comprehensive clarifying insights. It is full of love and all of a sudden it is all around us. It embraces us. It accepts us completely and unconditionally. It loves us, irrespective of what we have ever done or what we will ever do. And we feel completely unworthy to be present in this overwhelming perfection. The Light is all around us, but it is also within us. One person said that The Light is so wide-ranging that every single person is part of it, though just a very small part. It can be compared with a grain of sand on the beach: each human is like a grain of sand while The Light is the whole beach.[3] We are, as they tell us, part of One Big Whole. One person, however, told me that it was not that we are a part of this One Big Whole, but rather that the One Big Whole is part of us. This seems confusing, but the experience is ineffable and it is difficult to for people to find the right human words to express what is going on. In each case there was a feeling that there seems to be a great interconnection among all people, nature, and The Light. In fact we seem to be living in a kind of what I call a "Unity Universe."

The Life Review

In the presence of this fantastic, incredibly powerful, all-knowing, comprehensive, and unconditionally loving Light, there is the moment when some people see their life pass before their eyes, as if they are seeing a film. But this film is very peculiar. It is a panoramic, interactive experience. It is as if we can see everything from different sides. Moreover, it seems as if in the presence of this Light people become endowed with an enormous knowledge. As a result of this we can see all the details of our life, sometimes even details from before our actual birth. We see our childhood with our parents and our brothers and sisters, our time in secondary school, our first love, our marriage, our job, our everything … Everything is there.

During this life review we will not only see the facts, but we will also feel all the feelings linked to these facts, down to the last detail. Even our thoughts appear not to have been lost in the course of time. Each thought is there, each unexpressed idea about someone else. Everything has been stored and the complete picture is shown to us. We relive the happiness we experienced in joyful events during good times, but we also relive the sorrow of unfortunate events in the bad times of our life. We also see what we have done. We get to see our own actions, our own choices, and how we have come through difficulties.

That is not all. There is this interactive side to a life review as well. We will also feel how our actions are experienced by the whole world, by all other people, and by animals as well. This is all about the impact of our actions. We'll feel the emotions that we have aroused in others. And the peculiar thing is that we feel those emotions in the first person singular: "I feel those emotions, as if what I did to others is actually now done to myself."[4] In this way we will feel the joy and love we have given to other people and how those other people were delighted about what we did for them. We will feel very happy if we have done good and loving things, because it will be as if those good and loving things were done to us.

When we have had a friendly chat with a taxi driver, we'll feel his happiness chatting with such an interested passenger. If after our child's school day, we went over all the big and small events of that day with our child, we'll feel our child's profound happiness about such loving involvement. When we had a discussion with our colleague to clear the air, we'll feel his intense gratitude for the decreased tension. When we help people in need, we'll feel their joy from their perspective. All the feelings of happiness and joy that we give our partner, our children, our parents, our friends, our colleagues, and also our unknown fellow man, we'll relive down to the last detail. And we'll be glad and very satisfied that we did those things.

However, … in a similar way we'll also feel the impact of our negative, cold-hearted and indifferent actions on other people. We will feel the full impact of it on others. All the sorrow and all the pain we inflict on others, however small they may have been, will be felt by us in full detail with great intensity and with all nuances. We'll feel the impact as if those things were done to us. Our hurtful remarks towards the homeless person about his being an alleged nuisance will cut through our own souls. Our indifference to our partner's problems at work will give us a feeling of abandonment ourselves. If we were a thief in our real life, we'll feel the great sorrow we inflicted upon that unknown person by entering his or her house, turning it into a huge mess and taking his or her precious possessions. The same applies to the many years of pain we inflicted upon people. For instance, if we took the lives of their beloved ones during that robbery, or injured people from a bomb attack, or, for that matter, if we caused the loss of life and destruction from the 9/11 airplane impact on the World Trade Center, we will feel all the pain and suffering we caused. In general, we'll be able to feel every bit of pain we inflict on others, as if it is done to ourselves.

No Judgment

That we can feel everything we have done for others or to others as if it happens to us is a very remarkable "special effect." It is something a normal human being could not have perceived. This is so extraordinary, and in its way so unearthly, that it is actually unique. There is something else about The Light that is unique: the tremendous forgiveness and the unconditional love that is radiated from It. This is because even though we are completely defenseless as we see all the facts and feelings in and around our life as it passes by us, and even though we feel deeply ashamed of all those unkind actions, The Light does not change at all. It doesn't judge us. It remains totally loving. It remains full of understanding and full of forgiveness and it continues to accept us unconditionally, regardless of all our shortcomings and in spite of all the pain and grief we caused to others.

In the presence of this completely perfect and unconditional love warmly surrounding us, something happens within ourselves. We feel our own shortcomings. We assess all our actions and thoughts. We do that all by ourselves. No Bible is produced, no Koran is opened; no Bhagavad Gita, no lists of "do's and don'ts" is presented. No rabbi comes along; no priest, imam, Brahmin or lama is consulted. We literally assess ourselves in The Light of the complete love in which we are present at that moment, endowed with all knowledge about everything that was, and everything there is and shall be. We also see the place we have in this scheme and the tasks that we seem to have had on Earth.

Some people say that a sort of discussion begins about their life, although it's not in words, but in thoughts. Sometimes the discussion is conducted with The Light and sometimes with other beings that they encounter there. However, the discussion always lacks the blaming tone. Nobody is aggressive, and no one stamps his or her feet telling the NDEer how wrong he or she was. It is more like having questions put to them, such as: "Why did you do that?" "What did you think when you said this?" "Which second thoughts did you conceal from the other?" "And why?"

Distressful NDEs

With all the wonderful NDE stories, one could easily reach a euphoric state of mind because it is likely that we all will get these kinds of wonderful experiences after we die. This is true, but unfortunately people have also reported distressful NDEs. These range from having the feeling of some uneasiness to having sheer terror with visions of a hell-like environment. It is still not known what causes someone to have a distressful NDE. It seems easy to suppose that people who have had such an NDE would probably have done things "wrong" in life, but this conclusion cannot be supported by what we presently know about distressful NDEs. Although there are enough distressful NDEs to be sure that they are no statistical outliers, there are still too few to draw valid conclusions from.[5]

It should be understood that distressful NDEs can really be terrible. An important aspect has to do with communication. In the heaven-like NDEs the communication is easy and immediate and always full of love and understanding. However, in distressful NDEs there seems to be no constructive communication. There even seems to be an absence of it, causing people to feel completely alone. Without positive communication the total impression of the experience is one of isolation, loneliness, desolation, or even abandonment. Moreover, there is a feeling of rejection and hatred as well as a constant sense of danger and violence. There is a lot of fear and panic. Some even felt the presence of an evil being.

In an extraordinary book on this subject, Howard Storm describes his distressful NDE.[6] He encounters creatures that start to attack him and they seemed to have great fun. "They were playing with me just like a cat plays with a mouse." He says that the experience was far worse than any nightmare, because it seemed more real than being awake. To him it was "super-real."[7] Fortunately, there is a happy ending to his story. Based on this report and some other accounts, I think there is a general way out of these hellish experiences. I will come back to this idea in some of the following chapters.[8]

People who have had a distressful NDE have the same after-effects as people do who have had blissful NDEs. People in both of the NDE categories change thoroughly after their experiences and their lives subsequently turn around. And from both kinds of experience we can learn fabulous things.

Messages from Near-Death Experiencers[9]

Even though each NDE is unique and there is not one NDE equal to another, one can still derive recurring themes from them. I am convinced that acknowledging the wonderful messages from NDEs could make people happier. Moreover, if sufficient people would acknowledge these messages, we would have a "heaven on earth." Here are some of the messages from The Light that could make our world better.

We Are Profoundly Interconnected:
Focus on our Long-Term "Our-Interest"

Take a look at some of the remarkable things said by NDEers. They say that during their experience their knowledge expands infinitely. It is as if all knowledge is available to them and that they just have to tap into it. Time is no limitation. All time seems to be there at the same time. They are able to look into the future and see what is going to happen many years from now, just as they are able to look back in history. Space is no limitation either. By just thinking of a place the NDEers can be at that place if they like. The life review also gives the NDEers the possibility to feel exactly what they have done for others, and this feeling comes in a very direct way. They can feel it with such acute empathy that it is as if they themselves are the others. Apparently there is no division between them and the others.

All of this and much more indicate that we are profoundly interconnected and that we are part of something great. This is mentioned time and again by many NDEers. From this we can conclude that we are part of One Big Whole. We are living in a Unity Universe.

The consequence is that whatever we do or think, it has an effect on everything else. It is like tossing a stone in a pond. The effect of the stone is not limited to where the stone hits the water. The stone creates shock waves that go through the whole pond, both on the surface and down below. In this sense we have a creative power within us. We have the ripple-creating power. We should be aware of that power and try to create only positive ripples. Because if we do, we create positive energy in Unity Universe and in the end we will all benefit from it. Of course, the opposite is true for the less optimal things we do. Those things freeze energy.

The conclusion is that if we are so profoundly interconnected, we should do what is good to others and to nature because we in fact do this good to ourselves. Therefore, it would be best to change our focus away from our short-term self-interest and redirect it to the longer-term "our-interest."

Everyone Is Important

There are three simple reasons for this. The first follows from what has been already said. We all belong to a Unity Universe where we are profoundly interconnected. If I feel that I am important, then everyone else is important, too. If I feel that someone else is important, then I am also important.

The second reason is that everyone seems to have a task. You wouldn't be here on Earth unless you had a task to fulfill. During their NDE a lot of people understand that they have to go back to their physical body because they haven't completed their task. The interesting thing is that the moment they return to their body, they usually forget what that task was. Only a few people were able to remember what they had to accomplish. The task doesn't always have to be very compelling. It can be something ordinary and common, like raising children or working in a specific team. Probably there is not only one task we have to do. And certainly the overarching task is to practice love and compassion. In any case each task is important to Unity Universe, and we will come to appreciate the whole picture the moment our consciousness steps out of this life into the other part of Unity Universe.

The third reason why everyone is important is that each of us is part of The Light, or carries a part of The Light. That makes each of us immeasurably important. For that reason, there are no lesser souls. This appeared, for instance, clearly to an NDE of a woman who was brought up in a "dysfunctional family," as she put it herself.[10] She had suffered a lot and thought she was not able to change her situation. During her life review she was asked how she had honored the Divine Light within herself. Through this question she realized who she actually was; in her own words: a "true child of God." That was wonderful because it made her important, but it also came with a responsibility to respect and honor herself. We have to respect and honor ourselves because of The Light within us.

It means that we should try not to allow others to misuse or mistreat us physically or mentally. We should actively look for honorable solutions for everyone. More often than we think, there are honorable alternatives, in which quiet and peace are possible. They may sometimes not be easy to realize, but we have to try. By actively trying, we already show our respect for The Light.

Everyone Is Indispensible

We are absolutely important. Everyone is. But it is much more than that. Everyone's presence on Earth is required; we are indispensable to this world. This followed from the NDEs of some people who took a very drastic step when they faced mounting difficulties and felt that the world would be better off without them. Suicide is regarded by them as far from an optimal solution. All of those who have made a suicide attempt seem to be glad that they didn't succeed. None of them would ever try to do it again! Suicide was clearly no longer an option for them. In addition, those people were willing to counsel others against suicide.[11]

One NDEer who attempted suicide understood that her act was like throwing a stone in a pond.[12] The ripples would go over the entire surface of the pond. She understood that this would also be the case within Unity Universe. Since everything is thoroughly interconnected, her act would create ripples that would travel through the entire universe. She felt all the opportunities she would have in life and how her act would cause her to waste all those opportunities. It also meant to her that people who were supposed to meet her later in her life would not know her, and this felt like a serious loss.

Therefore, we should know that we are indispensable and should allow ourselves to cope with the problems and to come through. This is because when we do, either by finding a good solution or just with the passage of time, we will find ourselves in a new situation and our life will get better. In addition, we will have gained an experience and be wiser because of it. And we will have added something good to Unity Universe.

Life is a gift. NDEers say that killing ourselves is like rejecting a present, the present of life itself. You throw this present back in the face of Unity Universe, or God, who made it possible for us to live on Earth. The killing of oneself is thought, in essence, to be no different from the killing of others. By killing someone else, you take away the gift that was handed to that person. As one person put it: "You interfere with God's purpose for that individual."[13] Due to the profound interconnection of all and everything within Unity Universe, a gift to someone else can also be seen as a gift to ourselves. It means that each and every person around us also has a meaning for us and for our life, and in this way can be assumed to be part of the gift to us—even if the person is our enemy in earthly life.

Both suicide and the killing of others are no simple phenomena, and we should be careful in judging these. In some cases we may easily agree that it is wrong to kill or commit suicide. An example is the person who committed suicide after reaching the age of 65 in full health because this person didn't want to experience the degeneration phase of life (this is a real case!). Similarly, it is easy to say that it is wrong to kill someone just for the pathological pleasure of it or because the victim is a competing drugs-baron. Those are the extremes on the one hand. However, there are also extremes on the other hand.

What should we think of people who kill or commit suicide to save the lives of others? What about the woman who was hiding in a cellar in the war-torn city of Groznyy, Chechnya? She was summoned by her companions to stifle her crying baby herself or otherwise they would do it for her, since the crying might attract the Russian soldiers. If that happened they would surely all be killed with a hand grenade. She did what they urged her to do. Nobody would want to be in her situation.

And what do we think about people who kill or who commit suicide while being in the midst of severe mental depression? Who would not, for instance, feel sorry for the mentally unstable French grand chef de cuisine who committed suicide because there were indications that the Michelin Guide was going to reduce the number of stars awarded to his restaurant?

And what do we make of the people who jumped from the Twin Towers just before they collapsed? They were in distress and probably had to choose between death by burning flames or death by gravity. And what about active euthanasia in case of terminal illness, where there is no prospect of recovery, and where the patient suffers unbearable pain? And where is the line between this kind of euthanasia (or murder, as some people still call it) and the administration by doctors of ever-higher and eventual lethal doses of morphine to combat the pain? I wouldn't want to judge those situations, but I am absolutely convinced that The Light will look at all this with a greater deal of love than we ever could.

Returning Home Is Our Birthright

NDEers are convinced that our consciousness is eternal. It will not die. That is why they are no more afraid of dying. More than that, they long to be dead because they know they will go back again to that wonderful environment, which they call "home." One NDEer once told me: "Dying is the best part of life; I cannot wait to do it." Nevertheless, they generally know they shouldn't look for a way to get there "prematurely," even though they may suffer from severe "homesickness." They also learn to enjoy life in a different way. They have a greater desire to live life. Another NDEer told me: "I am not occupied with death, I am doing life!"

Here the important message is that our consciousness is eternal. The only thing that will die is our physical body, which we will discard as if it is a coat. This means that the moment we are born and we put on that physical body as if it were clothing, we receive the right to return back to the other part of Unity Universe. We can think of it as our birthright to go back to the environment where The Light is. The reason is that we all are a part of The Light; we all carry The Light within us.

This is also the case for people who have a distressful NDE. No one can be separated from The Light, because we all are a part of It.

Love Is the One Building Block

Of all the messages that NDEers give us, the most important one is that of love. They claim we are loved beyond our wildest imagination. The love from The Light is unconditional. Realize what that means. Unconditional means that there are no conditions. We don't have to do something in particular or to refrain from something in order to receive this love. It will be there.

In principle, this means that we can do whatever we want without taking notice of the needs of others and still be enveloped with all the love there is. But this wouldn't be fulfilling. We would become aware of our self-centeredness and would suffer from having missed the opportunities to develop compassion and to make other people happy.

Love and compassion are the only things we can take along with us when we die. These are the only things we can show to The Light. The treasure that we have acquired on Earth is the love we have given.[14] It is the Love in a very broad sense: for everyone and all of nature without distinction, and not only for our own family, our own clan, our nationality, our partners in religion or our own backyard. That includes both the lucky ones that have more and reach it with more ease than we do as well as the more unfortunate ones, like the man or woman in the street who begs for money. They are our equals. They are all our brothers and sisters. And it goes further, because it does not only have a bearing on the love for people, but also for animals, for all life, for the whole of nature and, therefore, eventually for everything around us. The reason is that in the end, everything physical or non-physical is equal to The Light (or God or whatever we desire to call It).

3

Hinduism

TAT TVAM ASI: THAT IS YOU

The Eternal Just Way

Hindus themselves say that they have 330 million gods. This then can hardly be called a monotheistic religion. It is also the main reason why Muslims throughout the centuries regularly clashed with Hinduism and still do today. But we will see that Hinduism is in fact more of a monotheistic religion than one would think.

Rightly so, Hinduism is considered a major religion. It is not only professed by the majority of the billion people living in India but also by the majority of the people in Nepal and a few enclaves elsewhere in the world, such as the Indonesian island of Bali. Due to migration of Hindus to other places in the world Hinduism became the religion of significant minorities in several other countries.[1] There is another important reason why this religion should be discussed here. Hinduism was the starting point for several other religions, such as Jainism, Sikhism, and Buddhism. The latter also became a major religion and is discussed in the next chapter.

The earliest form of Hinduism developed between 2700 and 1500 BC. That is the same period during which Stonehenge in England, the step pyramid of Djoser, and the big pyramids of Giza in Egypt were constructed. It is therefore really an old religion, perhaps even the oldest religion still in practice. However, it has changed a great deal so that it does not have the same form and content as it did then.

Hindus have their own name for their religion. They call it the "sanatana dharma," which is often translated as the "eternal religion," but means something more like the "eternal just way," or the "eternal correct conduct (or behavior)." Dharma, as we will see, is a very important concept. It is thought to be a law of nature, like the law of gravitation. In this case it is a law of cosmic order by which everyone is governed. Cosmic order is characterized by cycles, one of which is the cycle of life: everyone

17

who dies is born again. This repeating reincarnation only stops when we are able to escape this death-life cycle. A number of escape techniques are offered. However, just a few people are fortunate enough to have the time to follow these techniques. For all others the best thing to do is to behave correctly in order to obtain a better reincarnation. This requires the fulfilling of our duties that correspond with our present place in the world, which is determined by the social group that we belong to (the caste) and by our position in the family. In this way sanatana dharma focuses on the right behavior. This makes it possible for us to learn in this life that which is necessary for a better next life. So it is important to live a life of dharma, a life of righteousness.

From Three Hundred Thirty Million Gods to One God

The Vedic religion is characterized by a whole range of gods and goddesses who all have a specific task or a realm and who compassionately serve mankind. They come with wonderful stories and legends. It is traditionally said that there are 330 million gods. I couldn't trace where this very high number originated, but know that it is meant to approximate an infinity.[2] This is because Hindus treat every aspect of life as divine. Worship involving rituals, sacrifices, symbolic offerings, and chanting and music are as much a part of daily life as breathing. In cities and villages, in most houses, on estates and sawas, and near forests, rivers and streams, there are shrines and small altars. Hindus see God everywhere; He has many forms and is expressed in all that exists. The shrines and altars are not only erected for the few dozen popular gods, but also for the many unknown local wandering spirits and deities that people think they know or that show God's local divinity. In this way the incredible number of 330 million can be understood.

From the most recent religious texts we see three gods emerge who together form a Trinity. They are Brama, Vishnu, and Shiva, and each has his own specialty. Brahma is the god of creation. He creates the universe at the beginning of each new cycle in the way he did with our present universe. He created everything, including the gods and demons. Vishnu is the god of preservation. He preserves the order of creation. Finally, Shiva is the god of destruction. In the end he destroys everything again.

Originally the three gods were separate individuals, but Vishnu is said to have explained that Shiva, Brahma, and he are one. They only take

different names for the three phases in the universe: creation, mainte-
nance, and destruction. Something else he says in this context is also very
interesting. He says that as a trinity they are present in all creatures, and
that for this reason wise people see other people as their equals.[3] That God
is in everyone could be a statement of an NDEer. That everyone deserves
our respect is endorsed by all NDEers.

The 330 million gods have been reduced to only three, but we can
even take it one step further. The three gods also came from somewhere,
namely from the one Spirit Supreme, the never-created Creator, the One
who created the god of creation and gave him the sacred Vedas. That
Spirit Supreme is called Brahman. The Hindu priests are therefore called
Brahmanas or Brahmins, meaning "those that have to do with Brahman."[4]
The god of creation, Brahma, emerged from the left side of Brahman.
Then, in order to maintain what had been created, Vishnu emerged from
the right side.[5]

Upanishads: That Is You

In the Upanishads,[6] the sacred texts, a lot is said about Brahman. From
the beginning till the end Brahman is described in many different ways.
You might say that, like in the Koran, the Spirit Supreme has a lot of
magnificent names. In the Koran there are ninety-nine wonderful names
for Allah. In the Hindu religion there are probably at least as many for
Brahman. I already mentioned the "Never-created creator," but there are
many more.

I'll mention a few of them: the End of love-longing,[7] the Spirit of
Light, the Immortal, He is within all, and He is also outside,[8] the Radiant
Light of all Lights, Creator of the god of creation,[9] He is greater than all
greatness,[10] He is in all and He sees all,[11] He rules over the sources of
creation, from Him comes the universe and unto Him it returns,[12] the
God of love,[13] He is beyond time and space, and yet He is the God of
forms infinite, the Lord of all good, He is the home of your immortal-
ity (!), no one was before He was, and no one has rule over Him, He is
the source of all, He is pure consciousness, creator of time, all-powerful,
all-knowing, the loving Protector of all,[14] immeasurable, inapprehensible,
beyond conception, never-born, beyond reasoning, beyond thought, His
vastness is the vastness of space,[15] He is joy,[16] the beginning and the end,
life of all,[17] the Eternal.[18]

There are so many descriptions that the conclusion in fact should be that Brahman cannot be described. And actually, this is explicitly stated: words cannot reveal Him.[19] The reason for this is that His form is not in the field of vision and that no one can see Him with mortal eyes.[20] He cannot be reached by the senses, or by austerity or by sacred actions.[21] Therefore, it is safest to simply call Him the "ONE," and as such He is referred to regularly. See here the similarity with Judaism and Islam.

But now for the surprise. All these splendid names and all these unreachable qualifications, all that is … you. Brahman is in everything, and He is, therefore, also in you. That is you. In Sanskrit language: "Tat tvam asi."

The piece of Brahman in you has its own name. It is called the Atman. They are the same; they are equal, and despite the fact that one cannot reach Brahman or Atman with the five senses, there is another way to reach this ONE. It can be seen by a pure heart and by a mind and thoughts that are pure.[22] It can be seen indivisible in the silence of contemplation.[23] It can be reached by meditation and an ascetic lifestyle (by yoga) to control the senses. But I will come to that in next sub-section. First, we must understand Atman.

In a well known part of the Upanishads a father explains to his son how to see the equality between Brahman and Atman. He asks the son to place salt in a bowl of water and come back to him the next morning. The son does what he is asked to do. The next morning his father asks him to bring him the salt. The son looks in the water, but cannot find it any more. He is asked to taste the water from one side. It, of course, tastes salty. He is asked to taste the water from the middle. Again it is salty. And then from the other side. It is salty. Then his father says: in the same way you cannot see the Spirit, but in truth He is here.

An invisible and subtle essence is the Spirit of the whole universe. According to Hinduism it is also in you, in other humans, in animals, and in everything. When people greet each other in India, they press their palms together. It means that they greet this godly substance in you. That substance is you: Tat tvam asi.[24]

So Many Descriptions of Brahman, and They Are All In Us

Of course these splendid names and unreachable qualities are there to show the greatness of Brahman. They also resemble, however, the qualities of The Light in the near-death experiences. Most of the descriptions of Brahman can be found in the Svetasvatara Upanishad. Interestingly, at the end of this Upanishad it is declared that the teacher Svetasvatara had the vision of Brahman. Who knows, perhaps he was an NDEer…

And it is all also in us; we all have a part of Brahman in us. That sounds crazy, but when we go by the things some NDEers say, then maybe it isn't untrue. The Light seems so all-embracing that even we are a part of it, albeit a very small part. One compared it to a grain of sand on the beach: each human is like a grain of sand while The Light is the whole beach.[25] Another said that we are all children of God, and so we all too are little Gods. We just have to remember our divinity.[26]

Take this just a step further. Remember that NDEers say they could feel exactly what others felt. They could feel what effect their actions had on others as if they undergo these actions themselves. They felt what the impact was of positive actions, but also of negative actions, and they felt it down to the last detail. Remember also that NDEers say that their knowledge was increased infinitely as if they could tap into all the knowledge there is. Remember also that time and space form no limitations anymore. "All time exists at once." Because time seems not to limit us anymore, we can at the same time look back in history and see the present and the future. Space doesn't form a limit either: just think of a place, and we will be there. If we want, we can be everywhere at the same time.

All of this seems to indicate that there is a kind of "Unity Universe" and that we are an inseparable part of it. Through this Unity Universe we are profoundly interconnected with each other, but also with nature. This makes it possible to feel in great detail what others felt, to know everything there is to be known and to surpass space-time as we experience it in our four-dimensional world.

Upanishads: Escape from Reincarnation

Brahman fills everything with his radiance. Consequently, it is in each of us. Therefore our Atman is pure and untouched by evil.[27] It does not grow old and does not die, and no one can ever kill Atman, since it is everlasting. According to the Upanishads: "This is the real castle of Brahman wherein dwells all the love of the universe."[28] That all sounds very promising. However, despite these reassuring words we know all too well how this God within us, this Atman, goes astray. After all, we all do things that are not in alignment with its divine nature. How do we explain this?

Our Atman is usually compared with the lord of a chariot. On a chariot there is always a charioteer. In the comparison to our being, the charioteer is our reason. The mind is the reins. The chariot itself is our body. It is pulled by five horses that represent the senses.[29] It shows that our body houses our Atman, but that our spirit is under the power of pleasure and pain. In fact, Atman is ruled by the senses that cause pleasure and pain.[30] And that is exactly what the problem is. If our horses (our senses) are wild and rule us, our Atman will go astray. That is why we have to get control over the horses.

There is more to say about the senses. They give us the feeling that we are individuals. Whenever the soul has thoughts of "I" and "mine" it binds itself with its lower self.

We have to control our senses. Only when we are the master, will we be free. But free from what? Free from going from one death to the next.[31] Reincarnation is introduced. It is like "a caterpillar when, coming to the end of a blade of grass, it reaches out to another blade of grass and draws itself over to it, in the same way the Soul, leaving the body and unwisdom behind, reaches out to another body and draws itself over to it."[32] The cycle of rebirth is called "samsara."

Our death will lead us to a new life, but it will be one that is in accordance with our earlier lives and with our former works. How our thoughts were, we will become. How the quality of our soul is now will determine our future body. "According to how a man acts and walks in the path of life, so he becomes. He that does good becomes good; he that does evil becomes evil."[33] That is what is called "karma." It is the actions in our previous lives that determine our position in our present life.

KARMA

In Hinduism karma is seen as a universal moral law. This law is just as impersonal and certain as the laws of gravitation. The law prescribes that everyone will be reborn in a situation that matches his or her actions in their previous lives. This requires that these actions are registered and remembered and that we will later be confronted with them. In that sense it strongly resembles the life reviews that some NDEers have had (see chapter 2).

However, there seems to be a significant difference between karma and the life review from NDEs. Karma is important because it determines how we will reincarnate and in what circumstances we will have our new life on Earth. The primary importance of a life review in NDEs has nothing to do with determining how we will reincarnate. The life review is there to make the deceased conscious of his or her actions. Our actions and thoughts have an effect in universe. We are creative through what we do and think. It is this effect that we have had in universe that we should become conscious of. How did we affect others? How did they feel about what we did? How were their feelings? And how true were our feelings when we did what we did, because it is especially our true intentions that are of great importance.

The loving presence of The Light and its total forgiveness are essential for gaining this consciousness. In this respect learning from our own mistakes and from setbacks is very important for our growth. What we do not understand yet at this moment, we have to learn by making mistakes and by coping with setbacks. Everything has its valid reason, including all disasters and misery in the world and in our own life. At this moment we may not understand its meaning, but when we cross over we will.

Gaining consciousness and understanding is the primary importance of life reviews, and not how we will reincarnate. Besides, reincarnation does not emerge as an absolute certainty from NDEs. It is true that a significant number of NDEers do not rule it out (half the population of the research by Opdebeeck[34]) and even believe in it. But at the same time a significant number of NDEers have no specific feelings about reincarnation.

In any case, karma is an interesting notion, but it depends on how we interpret it. The meaning sometimes given to karma is that we have to work out what we have done in previous lives. In itself this can be seen as positive, for instance, when we grow by achieving a better understanding of what went wrong previously. In that sense it resembles the function of a life review in NDEs.

But there also are negative interpretations of the effects of karma. For instance, when someone contends that when we are born in a poor country, under pitiful circumstances in a lower social class, we should not complain because this circumstance is due to our own bad karma. This kind of negative reasoning can lead to horrible situations and in the section on foolish fixations some examples of this will be shown.

The big question for Hindus is how we can escape the cycle of rebirth, the samsara. The answer is through the higher wisdom, which comes down to inactivity. This sounds a bit vague, but it means that evil has to be abandoned and our senses have to rest; there has to be concentration of the mind and peace in our heart. When reason rests in silence, the supreme path begins and then we can start. This is called yoga, a Sanskrit word that refers to "control."[35] It is control over our body and mind, through asceticism and meditation. We could say that the dizzy rollercoaster race of the chariot has to be turned into a managed sightseeing ride. This means that, finally, the lord of the chariot has to gain control over the charioteer, the chariot, and the horses. Through the practice of austerities we become aware of our Atman, the lord of our chariot. This way of gaining control is called the "yoga of knowledge."

People who are active and run around to do their daily business will not reach control and, consequently, will not come even close to the state of consciousness, in which the senses are silent and Atman becomes free.[36] It is only for those who "in purity and faith live in the solitude of the forest, ... and long not for earthly possessions."[37]

What a pity. Most people, whether they want to or not, have to do some work to stay alive or to keep others alive. In this way, only people who can afford to sit down and do nothing but control the senses are able to escape the cycle of life and death. And even for these happy few there is a final hazard. They should make sure to die while being in such a controlled state of mind, because even if they lived an ascetic life full of meditation in a far away forest, if their peace of mind is disturbed at the moment of their death, then, sorry to say, they forego their Nirvana.

The Song of God

If we would strictly interpret the Upanishads, the escape from samsara is only within reach for the very few. Fortunately, after the Upanishads another view of how to reach samsara is revealed. This is done in the Bhagavad Gita, which translates as "The Song of God" or "The Song of the Lord Krishna" and which by now is seen as a kind of Bible for Hindus.

There is a war between two groups of cousins from the Bharata family. The setting is on the battlefield. There is a bowman whose name is Arjuna. Because there is a war he is supposed to drive around in his chariot drawn by horses and shoot the enemy. Since he cannot drive and shoot at the same time he has a charioteer. Somewhere in the story his charioteer, Krishna, turns out to be the eighth incarnation of no one less than the almighty god Vishnu, who on top of that also says that he is identical to Brahman.[38] He took the human form of the charioteer to bring his message to human kind. It is the discussion between both men that makes the Bhagavad Gita a remarkable text.

The war described in the Bhagavad Gita is thought to represent the battle within ourselves, the battle between right and wrong. At the start of the story the bowman realizes that in the battle he is going to fight his own family. Overcome with compassion for them, his eyes overflow with tears. He wants to back away from the battle, but then his charioteer delivers his message: He says that Arjuna should not consider the bodies he is going to pierce with his arrows, but the Atmans within the other people. They are never born and will never die; they are everlasting. Slaying the body does not harm the Atman of the victim. Just like someone who casts off worn-out clothes, the Atman will cast off worn-out bodies.[39]

So part of the message is that the Atman cannot be harmed. But the charioteer continues. He says that it would be wrong for Arjuna to back away from his duties. Everyone has his own duty in life and everyone is supposed to fulfill that duty with dedication. Not fighting is equal to failing to do one's duty.[40] Krishna adds to this that it is not only important to

Your Own Duty

Ghandi, the pacifistic Indian freedom "fighter," was a great supporter of the Bhagavad Gita. For him it is very important that people respect each other's duties.[42] He says that the duty of one person may be sweeping streets and the duty of another might be accountant's work. They are both important, at least before God. The street sweeper's work is important to have a clean pavement so people don't stumble or become annoyed by litter in the street. The accountant's work is important to get a good view of the financial position of a firm. He believes that God will judge the work of both by the spirit in which it is done, not by the nature of the work. The nature of the work makes no difference whatsoever. This is an interesting thought in a religion where people in the lowest caste are not respected, even when doing work that is important to society and even when they do their work with complete dedication.

That everyone has a task while being here on Earth is something we also find in NDEs. Some people who had an NDE are suddenly not allowed to go any further and are even told to go back into their body in order to finish their task. In most cases these NDEers do not have the faintest idea what that particular task might be. It could be sweeping streets or crunching numbers, and it could also be something else, such as raising kids or learning to deal with ailing parents. Whatever our task may be, it always is of great importance to Unity Universe. Therefore others should always respect it. In addition, we must always do it ourselves. In that sense there is a great resemblance to the concept of a task in Hinduism.

fulfill your duty, but that it should also be your own duty. It is better to do your own duty inadequately then to do someone else's perfectly.[41]

The problem with doing our own duty is that it involves action, and according to the Upanishads action binds us to the world and thus to samsara. Krishna, fortunately, knows that and he solves this problem for us. His solution is simple. Do your work well, but renounce the fruit of it. Accept your task as a fact of life and dedicate its results to God. This he calls "unattached action."[43] That kind of action will not hinder you in escaping samsara. To the contrary, it is the only way to reach that "big prize." It should, however, be combined with the worship of God.[44] Both the dedication of the fruit of your action to God and the devotion to God will lead you to Him. This implies the full surrender of everything you are and everything you do to God. Doing that will lead to the extinguishing of "I" and "mine."

Then you know that all beings and everything are one, a unity in diversity. You have no ill-will towards anyone, you are compassionate towards everyone, and you are not afraid of others; you don't cause any trouble to the world and the world will not cause you any trouble; you treat friend and foe alike and you are untouched by respect and disrespect; you have the same feeling for pleasure and pain, you feel equal with blame or praise, and you are content with your lot.[45] If all that is the case, you will shed all remaining karma. The Atman is the only thing that remains. It can then reunite with Brahman, and there it is at last: eternity!

After all that wisdom Arjuna heard he believes that he speaks with God and he becomes curious to see Him. Krishna allows it and gives Arjuna divine eyes, because with earthly eyes no one can see God. Then Arjuna sees "the splendor of a thousand suns to shoot forth all at once in the sky that might perchance resemble the splendor of that Mighty One."[46] But Arjuna sees more. He sees the whole universe in its manifold divisions as one in the body of God. He sees the diverse multitude of beings—the final resting place of the universe. And he concludes that Krishna is the Imperishable, Being, not-Being, and That which transcends even these.[47]

These texts are are perhaps difficult to comprehend, but they resemble somehow the descriptions of NDEs. In NDEs one also cannot view The Light with mortal eyes, and strange descriptions are also given about what one has experienced.

The Ramayana: The Tourist Version

The previous sub-section was about Krishna, the eighth incarnation of Vishnu. This section deals with the Ramayana, which is the song of the Lord Rama, the seventh incarnation of Vishnu. At first glance it seems more logical to write about someone's seventh incarnation and then about the eighth, but there are good reasons to reverse the sequence. One reason is that, strangely enough, the Bhagavad Gita (with the story of the eighth incarnation) is thought to be older than the Ramayana (with the story of the seventh incarnation). Another reason is that the Ramayana explains further "the innovation of the unattached action" given in the Bhagavad Gita.

After the Upanishads the Bhagavad Gita introduces an alternative to the yoga of knowledge. The innovation is that one can follow the yoga of action in combination with the yoga of devotion, which in fact will again lead to knowledge. This is not only accessible to the priests, but to everyone, even women and the people from the lowest caste, the servants. Part of this innovation is that everyone has a duty to do, and that it is better to do one's own duty than to do someone else's duty. The Ramayana confirms this and stresses the importance of living correctly, pursuing righteousness and putting one's own duty above all personal considerations or personal happiness. This is what is meant by following a "dharmic" life.

Dharma and the correct adherence to dharma is found everywhere in the Ramayana. At first glance the Ramayana is a tragic love story about prince Rama. Rama means "charming" so that prince Rama in fact means "prince charming."[48] The story is very popular and it forms a rewarding subject for theatre plays. When you are touring India, Bali, or any other Hindu environment, you will most likely have the chance to see the story on stage. But you should be aware that what you see on stage is just the core of the love story with the happy ending. Important parts that express the meaning of dharma are left out, because otherwise it would not be fit for tourist consumption. The real story in the epic poem is thus a bit more detailed. How could it not be when there are 24,000 verses?

Let's start with the tourist version. The tourist stage story usually starts with prince Rama going to a contest to win Sita as his future bride. Sita is a princess from a neighboring kingdom. Of course the contest is difficult and there are many contestants, but Rama wins the archery contest. In the original story it is not about archery, but the difficult task Rama is given to string the bow of Shiva. The bow is so heavy and so unmanageable that no ordinary man can do it. Of course Rama succeeds, because in the Trinity he is the colleague of the god Shiva.

There is great happiness, but the happiness is short lived. There is a villain. This is Ravana, the demon king. He also wants to have Sita and decides to kidnap her. This happens when Sita and Rama are in the forest and Rama is temporarily gone to hunt a deer.

When Rama finally discovers that Sita is gone, Hanuman comes along. This is the monkey god who needs help from Rama. After Rama has helped him, he helps Rama in return. Hanuman finds out that Sita is kept on the island of Sri Lanka. Together with other monkeys he builds a bridge by throwing enormous rocks into the water. When he arrives at the castle of Ravana, he is captured. Ravana wants to kill the monkey by burning him, but the monkey wrestles himself free and with his burning tail he jumps through the whole palace and sets it on fire. The defeat of Ravana comes when Rama kills him with the sacred arrow.

Finally Sita is rescued and returns to Rama. He doesn't want her back unless she proves that she is still pure and didn't have any unauthorized physical interaction with Ravana. She has to walk through a ring of fire and because she, of course, has been faithful to her true husband, she comes out of it without any burns. They live happily ever after.

Rama in Tree Bark

And now, here's an important part of the real story. A nice example of dharma is shown when Rama is on the verge of ascending the throne. His father, the king, felt his powers weaken and had to look for an heir to the throne. He had long been pleased by the righteousness and humanity of Rama. Moreover, everyone in the country loves Rama and he loves everyone. He is the nicest and the most popular guy around, a "diamond in the midst of pebbles," handsome of stature, intelligent, soft and kind with the weak and the poor, stern and inflexible with the wrongdoers.[49] Therefore, the king asks Rama to be his successor. Rama agrees and festivities are planned. The neighboring kings are all assembled and the city is decorated beautifully.

One of the evil characters in this part of the Ramayana is a woman. She happens to be a deformed person with a hunchback (in this way it is easier to accept that she is evil). She is the lady-in-waiting of the king's favorite wife. When she understands that the buzzing business in the city has to do with the preparations for the crowning of Rama, she immediately goes to her mistress. She tells her that the king decided that Rama should be the next king, not her mistress's son, Bharata. The king's favorite wife is delighted. Of course she accepts the king's decision, whatever it may be. Moreover, she sees all the king's children as her own, and that includes Rama.

The hunchback is astounded, but doesn't give up so easily and eventually convinces her mistress that it is all a cunning treachery. It had been decided that the son of her mistress was the one to become king. The king had promised this to the father of her mistress, the hunchback says. The king made this promise in order that her father would give him the permission to marry her. The hunchback claims to have been the only one to hear this vow. She adds to her plea that when Rama becomes king, her mistress would be nothing anymore. She would become an ex-queen of an ex-king. Even worse, she would probably be reduced to be a handmaid of Rama's mother.

It works. The king's favorite wife panics. The hunchback then reminds the queen that she had once revived the king on the battlefield. He had promised her two favors. The hunchback suggests strongly to use the two favors and ask for the banishment of Rama to the forests for fourteen years, dressed in garments made of tree bark, and also to install Bharata on the throne. So this happens.

When the king hears these two wishes from his favorite wife, he is devastated, but has no other choice than to fulfill them. Here is one form of dharma: keep your promises.

The king is too weak to tell Rama himself and therefore the favorite wife has to do that for him. Rama takes the message calmly, with resignation and in good spirits. He is even cheerful. He says that he is thrice blessed. He can carry out his father's command (it is his duty to obey him), make his brother king (because he thinks his brother desires it), and go to the forest (there he can live with saints and sages and work on his inner self).

This again is a form of dharma: we shouldn't focus on our own self-interest. Our own pleasure does not come first, our duties do. Also when everyone is against him leaving for the forest, his mind is determined to do so because it is his duty. Even when the sage tries to convince him that his banishment in fact is his stepmother's wish, he says that it is also his duty to obey her since she derives her authority from his father.[50]

Finally, when Rama wants to leave the palace he does so dressed in tree bark. He does this to show his new ascetic lifestyle. His wife Sita and his brother Laksmana come to join him, also dressed in tree bark. His brother does not want to stay in the palace with the new king and wants to follow Rama on his own account. Sita does so because it is her duty as a wife to follow him. So the three people wrapped in tree bark leave the city. When the king hears this, he dies in grief.

Bharata does not know anything about all this. He was out of the country visiting his grandfather, the father of his mother. Only when he gets notice that he has to come back to the palace, and hears that he is supposed to be king, does he become very angry with his mother. He calls her a serpent and an evil woman and says that he will spare her life only because Rama would despise him for taking it. He sets out to go to the forest to try to convince Rama that he didn't know of this treachery and to ask him to come back and become king. He does this, also dressed in tree bark. Rama refuses because it is his duty to realize the king's and his stepmother's wish.

DHARMA

The whole Ramayana is about dharma, i.e., the right way of living or the right way to act. If you read the story again, you will see all kinds of right ways of doing things. To mention a few do's and don'ts: we should not break promises, we should obey our father and (step) mother, and we should be decent; we should have devotion for gods, live ascetical lives, be truth-loving, and not kill if it is not necessary (interestingly, the deer killed by Rama poses a bit of a problem here). And these are a few qualities we need: righteousness, humanity, readiness for self-sacrifice, forgiveness, and compassion. And remember that the king chose Rama to be his heir because he is a "diamond in the midst of pebbles": he is handsome of stature, intelligent, soft and kind with the weak and the poor, and stern and inflexible with the wrongdoers. And the most important right way of living is that we have to be conscious of our duties.

Rama's duties had a great significance for humanity. They were determined by him as a god in heaven before he descended to Earth. He also determined the duties of his brother and wife, who were also gods before they descended to help Rama. Their duties were also predetermined in heaven and it was their task to act together so that Rama could destroy the demon Ravana. For that to happen, Rama and Sita had to be married, Sita had to be kidnapped, and Laksmana had to be Rama's helping hand.

Even though it may seem so, the predetermined duties are not there only for the gods. According to Hinduism normal people like us have duties as well, and they too are predetermined in heaven. The right way to act (dharma) is to fulfill our duties to the best of our ability. If we don't, we trespass against the cosmic law. There will be imbalance and we will harm ourselves and everything else in universe.

From NDEs we can also conclude that we have a purpose on Earth. We are here for a reason. We all have a special task to fulfill: to make a contribution to the world, to nature, and to the lives of others. We might call that a duty. This duty has been predetermined before we were born. In many accounts where NDEers do not want to go back, they are told or shown what the reason for their existence is. And sometimes they remember that they promised to perform a specific duty, after which they finally decide to go back. However, when they are revived and come around, they rarely remember what the duty precisely is. They are sure about having a duty, but simply can't remember it anymore.[51]

They normally say that love is very important. It is the "Number One Duty" in life. Other things that are mentioned are courage, honesty, responsibility, discipline, wisdom, faith, making this world a better place, and expanding our circle of compassion. This starts to sound like dharma. But all of this is still rather general. There seems to be something more specific and something individual to each of us, but I hardly know of anyone who came back and could clearly remember what it is. I expect that it doesn't always have to be something very compelling like slaying the demon Ravana in order to save humanity. I suppose it can be something like raising children, looking after refugees, or establishing a prosperous firm that can generate a means of existence for its employees, all of which are extremely responsible tasks.

All of our tasks are very important, even the seemingly insignificant ones, because everything in the universe is interconnected in a very clever way. Some NDEers have said that if they hadn't come back to Earth, other people would have missed their connections and could then not complete their mission or purpose in life. Remember what the person in chapter 2 in my discussion about "everyone is indispensible" said after her attempted suicide: "My actions were like stones tossed into a pond. They rippled out, crossing over the entire surface of the earth, forever affecting and changing the face of it."

Buddha as an Incarnation of Krishna

After the important seventh and eighth incarnations of Krishna, we have to give the ninth incarnation some thought. It forms a link between Hinduism and Buddhism. Hindus believe that Buddhism is derived from their religion, since Buddha is the ninth incarnation of Krishna. Krishna came back to Earth as Buddha to save humanity again. He wanted to test people by bringing a false religion into the world, one that rejected the ancient Vedas and the caste system.

It will come as no surprise that the Hindus consider Buddhism as a false religion. According to Hindus you can only escape samsara by adhering to the duties prescribed to your caste and sub-caste. Buddhism, however, rejects the caste system altogether. According to Buddhism you don't have to pay attention to outer appearances, such as performing all kinds of rituals. Those are not necessary for the escape from samsara. What is necessary is the search for peace within ourselves. Because of these differing thoughts, Hinduism rejected Buddhism and vice verse. And a severe collision is normal in a situation where two religions claim to tell the ultimate truth. That happened, and for this reason Buddhism was virtually banished from India within a few hundreds of years after Buddha (about 500 BC).

The Essence of Hinduism

Despite the fact that in Hinduism a lot of gods are worshipped, the essence is that there is but One Entity, One Substance, which is normally referred to as the Spirit Supreme. It is everywhere and it is in everything. It is also in you and me. You may also call it God, but the difference with the Judeo-Christian and Islamic God is that God (or Brahman) is not an independent entity outside of us. We also have something of that Spirit Supreme (Atman) in us and we should be respected for this.

The problem is that this divine essence within us is trapped. It is trapped in matter. And after our death it will be reincarnated in a new body and be trapped again. This sequence of entrapments will continue forever unless we make it possible for our Atman to escape this cycle of birth, death, and birth again. Escape is possible, but it requires a lot of effort.

One possible means of escape is by acquiring knowledge. It is not scientific knowledge, but it is the knowledge of the Spirit Supreme. This knowledge can be acquired by rigorous asceticism and intensive meditation that should silence the senses so that the divinity within us can be heard. This requires that one should retreat from active life. However, living an ascetic life full of meditation is very difficult and the problem is also that it is impossible for everyone to do it at the same time. There have to be people who look after our food and shelter, who clean and protect us, and who look after our children and the elderly. Therefore, an alternative was presented which allowed for an active life.

The alternative prescribes that everyone has a duty and that everyone should fulfill that duty with dedication. We are allowed to be actively busy with working and caring, but we have to dedicate all the fruits of our action to Brahman. We should not be proud of our successes, nor should we be saddened by our failures. By doing this we will not act for our own benefit or for our own shallow self-interest. Apart from dedicating the fruit of our actions to Brahman, we should also worship Brahman by performing the correct rituals. This combination also leads to knowledge of the Spirit Supreme. Through this we could at least obtain a better next life and could possibly even escape from the cycle of life and death.

Foolish Fixations

The most striking foolish fixation is not the caste system in itself, but the way in which it is brought into practice. This results in serious discrimination and maltreatment of people. The caste system is derived from two important religious concepts, each of which is perhaps not completely incorrect. However, the way in which these notions are combined and then put in practice is harsh and heartless. Because the practice was never really challenged or questioned, it was allowed to develop further and was perfected to foolish extremes.

The two religious concepts referred to are karma and duty. Karma comes from the belief that everyone has had many previous lives and therefore will already have built up a record of service. A good record will imply a good karma that will be reflected in a more favorable reincarnation. A bad karma will do the opposite. The second concept means that everyone on Earth has a task to fulfill.

Developing the idea of karma has led to the caste system, because through this system karma can be materialized. You can then see from someone's position how he has previously performed on Earth. This combined with the concept of duty, however, has led to immobility within the system. The reason is that you should resign yourself to your own fate, which was created by yourself in previous lives. You have to live the life of your caste as well as possible. Only when you do that to the best of your ability will you be able to move yourself up the ladder—that is, not until after your death. Only then might you be promoted to a higher sub-caste within the present one, or maybe even promoted to the next, higher caste.

In time this harsh and heartless conviction has developed to extremes and the practice is revolting. People from higher castes look down on people from lower castes, and everyone looks down on people who don't even belong to a caste, the so-called outcastes or untouchables. These are shunned like the plague; they are insulted and they may not enter temples and houses of people with castes. In restaurants it is not uncommon that they even get a separate set of cutlery. The reason is that they do the dirty work, the work that has to do with impurities that can bring them into contact with blood or feces (tanners, toilet cleaners, sewer workers, cremators, undertakers, and the job of clearing away dead animals from the street). They lead the life of slaves, and they have done so for more than a thousand years.

There have been awful excesses. There was a time, not too long ago, when outcastes would wear bells that would warn other people of their approach. They could be beaten if their shadow touched a Brahmin. And even today there are many incidents when outcastes are assaulted. I have seen pictures of men with disfigured faces because of the acid that was poured over them. They had just been fishing in a pond owned by someone from a higher caste. There was another man with his legs missing as a result of a beating by people from higher castes. He had complained that the village chief hadn't paid for his construction services. There are women who have been burned alive in their homes or raped in front of their husband[52] just because their husbands, and maybe even they, themselves, have resisted the suppression. These are not rare incidents. They happen frequently and the stories can be read in newspapers on a weekly basis.

The caste system is not formally acknowledged. Nevertheless, it exists, is practiced, and people cannot escape membership in it unless they move to a city where it is easier to live an anonymous life. But even then their name or profession will disclose their caste. Membership of a caste is hereditary and being outcaste is hereditary as well. At present there are more than 160 million outcastes, which equals about half of the population of the United States or Europe.

The other foolish fixations that I want to mention also have to do with the way in which Hindu life has been organized. A woman's status is derived from her husband's. When he dies, she becomes inauspicious. It is thought to be sinful to survive the husband since it would have been better if she had died before her husband, or at least at the same time. And actually that is what regularly happened. Women took their own lives, and the most dramatic form of doing so was to jump onto her husband's funeral pyre. This practice is called "sati" after Shiva's wife who committed suicide by jumping into the flames. Sati was ashamed because her father had insulted Shiva. The reason? Her father had forgotten to invite Shiva to a dinner party.

The practice of sati supposedly started somewhere halfway in the first millennium after Christ. Often this suicide, or "self-immolation" as it is sometimes euphemistically called, was involuntary. The family insisted on self-immolation to protect the family honor, or just to be able to get hold of the estate. Although in modern India sati is prohibited, it still happens occasionally. A big controversy arose as recently as 1987 when a young 19-year-old widow, who had been married for only seven months, performed sati. According to one account it was voluntary because she calmly recited prayers while the flames consumed her. I fail to believe this story because to my knowledge it is a normal reaction to be screaming and not to be calmly reciting prayers. Another account, therefore, seems more probable: she was drugged and thrown onto the fire.[53]

↜ 4 ↝

Buddhism

DO IT YOURSELF: DISCARD THE "SELF"

There Is No Almighty One

Emperor Ashoka had won the war in Kalinga (India) in around 265 BC and he viewed an endless battle field that was drenched in blood. One hundred thousand people were killed. In addition, about one hundred fifty thousand people were taken away to live in captivity. He would later understand that they too had probably perished, meaning that his war had cost the lives of hundreds of thousands of people. He saw what a terrible thing he had done and he was overwhelmed with remorse.[1]

This all happened just sixty-one years after other enormous massacres, namely the ones that Alexander the Great caused in Asia Minor, Syria, Egypt, Babylonia, Persia (the greatest empire the world until then had known), and India. But whereas Alexander could only be stopped in his fanatic pursuit of world domination by his soldiers who refused to go any further, Ashoka was stopped by his own remorse. The terrible sight of the blood-soaked earth and the realization of the consequences of the aftermath of his war changed him. In his famous thirteenth edict and longest edict cut into rock he would publicly declare that he regretted this war, the massacres, and the enslavement. He declared that he would never do that again and that he hoped that his successors wouldn't think of doing such a thing either. Moreover, he stated that the real conquest is the conquest of the heart and he vowed to devote himself to that cause for the rest of his life.

Under his rule Buddhism thrived and soon became the major religion in India, almost totally replacing Hinduism. It would also find fertile soil in other areas, such as Sri Lanka, Tibet, Thailand, and China. But Buddhism would start to dwindle in India from the 7th century onward. The reason for this decline is uncertain. It would receive the final blow in 1193 when the Muslim Mohammed Ghuri conquered Bihar and killed all the "shaved idolaters."[2] By then the religion was thriving in almost all of the rest of East Asia.[3]

Buddhism had originated in India somewhere in the sixth or fifth century BC when Siddhartha Gautama, the future Buddha, was born. Since at that time all of India was Hindu, Gautama was a Hindu too. For this reason Buddhism is strongly influenced by Hinduism and uses the same concepts like karma and the idea of reincarnation. One important concept was, however, not adopted, which is the belief in Atman (or an individual soul).

In Hinduism the highest obtainable goal is the reunion of Atman with Brahman (the One Almighty Entity). In the Judeo-Christian tradition and in Islam the highest obtainable position is in heaven close to the Almighty One, whatever name this entity may have. In Buddhism nothing of that kind is possible. The simple reason is that the position of Almighty God or a Brahman is vacant and can never be filled. The position does not even exist.

Despite the lack of one Supreme God there are many gods, and it is possible for everybody to become one. However, it is not a position all would want to have. Although gods have a more pleasant life than any other being, they are only one of six forms in which people can be reborn. And, more importantly, gods are perishable. After a usually quite lengthy period, gods cease to exist and have to go through the same rebirth procedure that ordinary humans go through. Their reincarnation could be as a god, but it is more likely to be as one of the other forms available. Moreover, it is probably going to be in a lower form than the human one.

Therefore being a god is not the highest level attainable in Buddhism. There is something else. The best state human beings can achieve is to become enlightened. This means that there will be no more new lives. There will be no rebirths and thus no further suffering in any new life-form. And we can achieve enlightenment ourselves. In principle we don't need any higher power or anyone else to guide us. However, the road towards enlightenment is a difficult and long one. Fortunately there are those who have gone that road before and can tell us how to travel. These people are the buddhas. Buddha means "he who is enlightened." The most famous one is Siddhartha Gautama. After he turned into a buddha he became known by the name Buddha Shakyamuni, which means the Wise One or Sage or the Competent One of the Shakya clan. He is the founder of the religion we know as Buddhism. After he became Buddha, he remained on Earth to teach us how to follow him into this state of enlightenment.

What strikes me in Buddhist teachings is that Buddhism, in a way, is a very gloomy and depressing religion. In this terrible world of appearances we constantly suffer. We are kept in our world because of our cravings and desires, but also because of our great ignorance. Without that ignorance we would try to get out. However, if we would finally come to our senses and would really start to attain freedom from this life, we would discover that it will take eons and eons to reach our goal. The reason for this is that only as a human are we able to work on our progress towards enlightenment. Buddha, according to the Dalai Lama, once said that the chance of becoming a human again in our next life is equal to the chance of a blind turtle surfacing in the ocean with his neck exactly in the hole of a yoke floating somewhere in that ocean.[4] Oh, and I forgot to mention that this turtle surfaces only once in every hundred years ...

Buddha the Victor

Siddhartha Gautama was born a prince, but soon found out that he desired to escape from being reincarnated over and over again. Following the ancient customs of Hinduism, he retreated and started living an ascetic life. He did this rigorously. He lived on one grain of rice or one sesame seed a day, and it is even said that he tried to hold his breath to use as little oxygen as possible.

After a while he realized that this was not the way. By austerity and asceticism one cannot escape reincarnation and achieve enlightenment. He understood that one should follow the third way, neither the way of physical and emotional self-indulgence, nor the way of asceticism, but a way between these that would be best. Not surprisingly, his way would become famous as the "Middle Way."

For five or six years he practiced "mindfulness," which means that he observed all he did and analyzed all his feelings during each activity. He became aware of the way he walked, the way he talked, and the way he did everything else. He discovered that each desire that was satisfied would be followed by a new desire. Each craving was followed by a new craving.

He saw how human beings live from one moment to another and slowly change as a result of their decisions along the way. During this process they feel happy when one desire is satisfied, but unhappy again when a new desire pops up. In fact there is a continuous stock of desires and consequently there is continuous suffering.

Although the discovery of a multitude of desires was important in itself, he also discovered a peculiarity about some of those desires. He found that some can only be satisfied to the detriment of other people or even animals. People always want to be in a better position than others or want to have more than others. There is a special kind of suffering that comes from not satisfying these desires.

GRANTING OTHERS A BETTER SITUATION

In economics it is usually assumed that people make rational decisions. However, behavioral economics has demonstrated that this does not occur in reality. As an example, the following question was asked to a number of students: What would you rather have? Would you prefer to have an annual income of 50,000 pounds while others have an annual income of 25,000 pounds, or would you rather earn 75,000 pounds while others earn 100,000 pounds? Significantly more students chose the first possibility with a lower income for everyone and where they would also have a lower income of only 50,000 pounds rather than 75,000 pounds. They liked the situation that they would earn more than the others. Apparently they didn't want to grant a higher income to others.

NDEers would do this test completely differently. They would probably choose others to have a higher income that they would have themselves. After their experience they generally care less about money and more about the general happiness and wellbeing of others. And if that can be obtained by others having a higher income than they themselves have, so be it. They don't care about status, or about being in a better position compared to others. And least of all, do they want to satisfy their desires to the detriment of others.

Of course Buddha didn't know of these kinds of studies published about 2,500 years after his death, but he apparently did understand the basics of this peculiar psychological human motive. He apparently understood that continuous suffering is caused by desire, and he wondered what constituted desires.

He found the answer to be our egoism, stemming from the idea that we are something with an identity. Now he had the solution! He was going to discard that identity, that "self." And he would do that during four stages of his meditation.[5] In the first stage he would extend a huge, expansive and immeasurable feeling of love and friendship towards all creatures and direct it to all four corners of the earth. Then in the second stage he would cultivate a feeling of empathy with those creatures who were suffering. This would be the "easy" part of compassion: sympathy with someone who is in a less comfortable position. The more difficult part of compassion would be the cultivation of empathy for those people who are happy and in a more comfortable position. This kind of sympathetic joy is important in the third stage of the meditation. The final stage was the most difficult. It was the stage in which he would not feel pain or pleasure himself or for anyone else. This would be a feeling of total equanimity towards others.

The thorough practice of this kind of meditation would tear down the defenses of the ego and would make us feel united with everything and everyone. It was a very long learning process for Siddharta, but eventually after five or six years, when he was 34 years old, he felt that he was ready for this last state of meditation.

When he sat down under a sacred tree, he made a vow. He would stay there until he reached his goal. That lasted for 49 days, and if you think that it was a quiet and peaceful time, you are quite wrong. Mara, the leader of the demons and the enemy of the right way of reaching the end of the cycle of reincarnation, came to disturb Siddhartha and to prevent him from becoming enlightened and a buddha. Mara is always presented as a separate entity, as a demon, but it is also thought that he represents the bad part of the "self," in this case, the self of Siddharta.[6]

At first Mara tried to disturb him in a subtle way. With his three sensual daughters he tried to break Siddharta's concentration. The women tried to seduce him, but he didn't react. Then they tried to frighten him by sending deformed and distorted creatures to run and bounce around him, while making a lot of noise. When they discovered that this did not move Siddhartha even a little bit, they started to throw all kinds of things at him like axes, rocks, trees, and burning logs. However, by means of his utmost concentration, Siddhartha managed to transform all of these things into wonderfully scented flowers and lotus petals.

Mara was enraged. He screamed: "Get off my place. It's mine."

Siddhartha answered: "Mara, you have done nothing to reach knowledge, nothing for the well-being of the world or for enlightenment. This place of knowledge belongs to me; here all the bodhisattvas of the past reached enlightenment."

"But who will be witness to the dedication of your previous lives and of your generosity?" Mara suggested.

Siddhartha with his right hand reached out and touched the earth. The earth thundered: "I am witness."

This was the defeat of Mara and the victory of Siddhartha, who at that moment reached nirvana and became Buddha.[7] This dramatic moment of Siddharha touching the ground is often depicted in Buddhist art. One can still visit the place where the victory took place. There is even a Bodhi tree there, which is said to have descended from the original tree.

An interesting aspect about the emergence of the new Buddha is that he said: "It is liberated." He didn't say: "I am liberated," because that would not be possible. His "self" had disappeared and Buddha is not only one with himself, but also with everything else that there is. He had achieved an ultimate ecstasy, and in nirvana he discovered an immeasurable dimension of his humanity that he had not known before.[8] He would always refuse to describe or define the nirvana because there are no words to describe this feeling or these dimensions that he had discovered. It is within us. It is a place where one can go to have the ultimate peace of mind. It is there even when we are confronted with a lot of painful things. It can be a refuge. And importantly, according to Buddha it is there not because a greater power created it or allows you to go there. It just is there. Period.

Nirvana

Even though Buddha doesn't want to describe or define nirvana, what he says about it is interesting. It reminds us very much about what NDEers say. They say that there is an immeasurable dimension added to what we already know. That extra dimension is very close by as if it is around the corner. It is all around us, but it is also in us. It is there always, whatever happens.

Buddha says that we can always reach it. That seems to be inconsistent with what NDEers say. They long to go back to that feeling and to that extra dimension, but they do not know how to reach it again. Although they can of course reach it through death, they generally don't want that to happen because they want to finish their task or they want to add something positive to the world. Buddha, however, says that we can reach that dimension when we are still alive, although the requirement seems to be that we have to be enlightened to achieve this.

The Four Noble Truths

The big question is how to reach the state of enlightenment and thus nirvana. The answer for Buddhism is to follow the four noble truths. The first two noble truths explain to us what suffering is and analyze its cause. The last two tell us what we should do to eliminate the cause and thus how to end the suffering.

Suffering takes all kinds of forms. It begins with birth and ends with death, and of course there is a lot of everything in between. Traditional Buddhism has defined suffering as birth and old age, sickness and death, grief, sorrow, and despair, physical and mental pain, involvement with what one dislikes and separation from what one likes, and, finally, not getting what one wants.

It could be that we do not have or do not own something that we desperately want to have, like water or food or a Rolls Royce. This wish to possess does not have to relate only to material things. It can also relate to the wish to have a particular girlfriend or boyfriend, or to have a partner in general, or a specific job. It may also be that we have something that we'd rather not have, like cancer. Being separated from what we love is suffering, too.[9] We'd only get depressed extending the list of sufferings, so let's turn to the second truth, which analyses the cause of suffering.

It is important to know what the cause of suffering is, because if we do we can start to eliminate it. Knowing the cause of suffering is the second noble truth. Suffering, according to Buddha, is simply caused by yearning and desire. It hurts when we yearn for or desire something that we don't immediately get. When you don't get it at all, then the yearning and desire are certainly painful.

Where do the yearning and desire come from? The answer is: from attachment. It can be attachment to things, or to a person, to our job, to life, to the ideal of having a partner or to any other idea or concept. Any attachment causes great pain because it costs a lot of energy to try to get the object of that attachment if we don't already possess it; and if we do have it, it costs us a lot of energy to hold on to it. Since life changes constantly and is thus something unstable, we can never really be sure about what we have. In the same way instability may be the reason that we'll never reach what we are aiming for. The conclusion, therefore, is that any attachment in an unstable world causes pain.

Attachment arises from our own mind with the perception that it is an individual mind. The individual perceives himself and perceives others. So he sees a dichotomy: himself and others. The individual can therefore say: I want a Rolls Royce, I want food, don't hurt me, don't leave me, I need you, this job is mine, I hate you, I love you, and so forth.

The third noble truth provides the remedy to suffering and it is very simple: do not get attached to anything anymore. Stop attachment. Stop any yearning and desire. Then you won't get hurt when you can't reach your goal or when something is taken away from you. Stopping attachment in fact means terminating the concept of the "self" which is part of a world with duality, where there is "me" and "the others." Attachment comes into being when the "self" or the "me" desires something—like that job, that beautiful car, that partner, or when the "self" does not want to be ill, or doesn't want to be separated from a lost child. So if we are aware of that "self," which is the cause of the yearning and desire and thus the cause for suffering, we can also discard it.

The fourth noble truth shows us how to discard the "self" and, no, it is not through suicide. It is by following the eightfold path, which is the core of the four noble truths. It is extremely important for reaching enlightenment. It shows us the eight ways to act correctly. Keep in mind that the word "correct" should not be interpreted as the opposite of "incorrect," but as "complete" and "perfected." So these eight paths are what it is all about. For instance, we should be free of malice, gossip, and lies, and abstain from harming any living being, avoid work that might harm others, try to produce good karma, and practice good meditation.

Buddha doesn't really speak about the termination of the "self." Rather, he denies that the "self" really exists. It exists only because of desires. But even then the "self" is not a stable entity. Buddha compares it to a blazing fire, which is also never the same. The "self" has some personality, but it changes constantly, from one moment to the next. This is caused by changing desires. When one desire is satisfied, another is created and the "self" strives to satisfy that new desire. That is the blazing fire.

Buddha tries to make clear that by holding onto the "self" we are in fact holding onto a very limited view. It is an extremely selfish point of view. And for that reason it is very curative and healing to realize that the "self" needn't be maintained or defended or even increased at the expense of others. This can be seen as an important part of the eightfold path.

ATTACHMENT

It is clear that according to Buddhism attachment is something bad. It prevents us from reaching enlightenment. Now it is very interesting to recall that with NDEs there is the possibility of having hell-like visions where people become stuck somewhere in the middle of material and spiritual existence. They cannot go back to Earth because they lack a body, but neither can they go forward into the spiritual world. The reason might be that they have been too materialistic and greedy and have had a very self-centered view of the world without recognizing the needs of others. They are too attached to their ego or to the material world and consequently seem to be unable to find their way to the spiritual world. They try to maintain the ego, and in doing so they cannot progress towards The Light. The remedy is to let go of our ego because the ego, according to NDEers, is less real (if it is real at all) than The Light.

UNITY UNIVERSE

Knowing that the "self" does not really exist is very important in Buddhism. It is an illusion that is maintained because our senses make us believe that it exists. However, if we hold on to the "self" we are in fact holding onto a very limited view.

There is a great similarity between this and what NDEers tell us. After their experience NDEers are convinced that they belong to something so much bigger. They know they are part of One Big Whole that I call Unity Universe. They feel their interconnectedness with everyone else, with nature, but also with that other world that we cannot see. Some people say they are enveloped in The Light and they even say they are one in and with that Light. Others see The Light everywhere. It is in front of them, behind them but also in them. They are part of it. All of this should lead to the conclusion that there is no "self." We are all One.

The feeling of this profound interconnectedness with all there is ends the moment NDEers return to their body. The body is a very confining structure, which some of them call a prison, a shell, or a wet suit that feels just a tiny bit too small. It gives people the idea that they have an identity, that there is a "self," but NDEers know that it is just an artificial separation from Unity Universe. In reality we are still profoundly interconnected, even when we live in this wet suit.

Karma

Karma is sometimes wrongly interpreted as fate, but it has nothing to do with that.[10] Fate is something that comes to us. It is something external. It is something we cannot influence. Karma is something different. We can influence it, but before I explain how that can be done, we should know that karma is thought of as an impersonal and natural law. It is a special case of the law of cause and effect. It is a universal law, just like the law of gravitation. Karma can be seen as the spiritual form of the law of cause and effect, which has to do with human lives. Since nothing can exist by itself and everything is based on some previous cause, our present life is based on what has happened in our previous life (or lives).

Every action in our previous lives leaves an imprint on our most subtle spirit. It is like seed in a field. It stays there until it is time to sprout. Our present life is the result of some or all of our actions in our previous lives. The seeds that do not sprout in this life will certainly do so in one of the next ones. The actions in our present life will form new seeds that will be added to the seeds that have not yet sprouted. This is why it is so important to accumulate good actions. They will lead to good things in our next lives.[11]

This means the most urgent thing we have to do is to concentrate on performing virtuous actions. The next most urgent thing to do is to create a permanent peaceful and positive state of mind. We never know when we might die, so we should always be prepared for it by never being in a state of anger, hatred, jealousy, or any other negative emotion. We should always remain calm even when something worrisome happens. Those worrisome times will pass. They are like waves that rise from the sea but that will eventually flow back into it again.[12] There is no power on earth, in heaven, or elsewhere that can put us in hell, except our own negative emotions.[13] They are very powerful, so we have to take care as to how we express them.

After our death, karma affects our soon-to-be-created identity. This identity depends on our actions in previous lives, and on the seeds that are there to sprout. This will continue as long as there is karma left to create a new identity. This means that an end is possible, namely when all karma has been exhausted and nothing is left. This will happen when we have discarded the "self," which is only possible by following the four noble truths and living a perfected life.

KARMA AND THE LIFE REVIEW

Karma can be compared with a list of all good and bad things we have done. Every action leaves an imprint on our most subtle consciousness and in that way it is retained. From the life reviews of NDEers it becomes clear that everything they have done throughout their lives is kept. Every action and even every word and every thought, however insignificant it may have been, is still there and can be shown to us. As a method of this complete registration, karma and the life review strongly resemble each other.

As will be shown later, karma is used in Tibetan Buddhism for the evaluation of our life. That corresponds with the self-judgment in NDEs. Although many people with an NDE are convinced that reincarnation exists, it is not clear whether the life review will be used to determine our future place on Earth.

KARMA AND THE RIPPLE EFFECT

Karma as the spiritual form of the law of cause and effect has some resemblance with the ripple effect that we know from NDEs. It was concluded that we live in a Unity Universe, where everything is profoundly interconnected. This means that everything we do and think has an effect somewhere else. Our actions and thoughts create ripples that travel through the seen and unseen part of the Unity Universe. In Hinduism the idea is that everything we do and think is kept in our karma and will exert its influence over our next life. In NDEs, however, the ripple effect is not limited to us in our next life. The ripples can be felt everywhere in the Unity Universe. If reincarnation exists, the ripples may be felt in our next life, but we don't know. What we do know is that NDEers say they saw their ripples traveling everywhere. They even affect places and people they don't presently know, or places and people they will never know during their earthly life. In that sense the ripple effect is different

The Tibetan Book of the Dead

Today's most famous Buddhist is the Dalai Lama, the leader of Tibet who has received the Nobel Peace Prize for his consistent resistance to the use of violence in his people's struggle to regain their freedom. Since his teachings can be found in all bookshops and have increased the interest in Tibetan Buddhism, it is appropriate to give this form of Buddhism some more thought. The Dalai Lama says astonishingly loving things, in spite of being embedded in a lot of Buddhist dogmas. His central creed is compassion. He even says that the most important property of Buddha is compassion.[14]

Not only have the wonderful teachings of the Dalai Lama received a lot of attention, but also The *Tibetan Book of the Dead* has been widely acknowledged. The title was given by the European editor who found the book in a Darjeeling bazaar, translated it, and published it in 1927. The original name is *Bardo Thös Grol Chen Mo: The Book of Liberation by Hearing in the Intermediate State*, although it has also been translated as *The Great Book of the Natural Liberation through the Understanding in the Intermediate State*.[15] It is regarded by many people in both the East and the West as an important text about the afterlife.

The *Bardo Thös Grol* concerns the intermediate state, where people dwell when they are dead and waiting to re-enter into a new form of life. It is supposed to give a road map that we can use when we are lost in the intermediate state looking for a way out, hopefully into nirvana, but more likely into a new life form. Throughout the book the deceased person is explicitly summoned by his name and told not to panic, but to listen to the instructions and to follow them. The idea is that although the deceased can still hear and see us, they cannot communicate with us. The text should therefore be read out loud to the deceased person.

The book was written in the 8th or 9th century by the great Buddhist teacher Padma Sambhava, who then buried it. A treasure hunter found it again in the 14th century. Where the writer acquired his knowledge is difficult to say, but I think it is unlikely that he had an NDE himself. Perhaps he had spoken to someone who had one, but in that case he put in a lot of his own interpretations on top of the original accounts of the NDEer. Even though the book gives very confusing descriptions of the phase of death, it also has interesting aspects, so let's see what it is all about.

After Disintegration There Is Integration

In *The Tibetan Book of the Dead* there is a description of how our present identity disintegrates until we have been reduced to the one indestructible drop of "energy-spirit inseparable from the clear-light transparency,"[16] whatever that may be. It resembles the "Atman" of Hinduism, although it is not thought to be part of one big all-encompassing entity like Brahman.

Then, based on our karma, a new identity is created with which we will be born again in a new life-form. The period, during which it is determined what our future will look like, is the intermediate state and is called the "bardo." This moment between the dissolving of our present identity and the building of our next identity is the most important phase. It is a kind of liquid phase between two solid phases and it is the phase where some influence can be exerted. In *The Tibetan Book of the Dead* itself, this is vividly compared with a gigantic tree trunk, which cannot even be moved by a hundred men. But when the tree trunk is in water, it is very easy to turn in any desired direction.[17] So the message is not to let this extremely important intermediate state just pass by.

The dissolving of our present identity comes in eight stages. To me it is amazing how detailed the description is. It almost seems scientific except for the lack of proof. I will present it just as it was described, with the terminology that to me is sometimes incomprehensible. In the first four stages the four elements are dissolved. These are earth, water, fire, and air. From this moment on the "coarse physical elements" are gone. The next thing to go is the "coarse consciousness," which is dissolved in the fifth through to the eighth stage, leaving only the "very subtle consciousness."[18] This starts with the fifth phase. The white cognition drop (the male essence) descends from the brain through the cognition channel towards the hart chakra. We then get a sense of white moonlight. After that, in the sixth stage, the red cognition drop (the female essence) ascends from the sex wheel towards the hart chakra. This gives us a sense of orange sunshine.

The seventh stage is the "black almost-attained"[19] stage that has also been called the "black full-attainment"[20] stage. In this stage both the white and red cognition drops entrap our consciousness. Our senses see black clouds or a black light. Then, finally, the real moment of dying comes with the eighth stage. This is the stage where we can see the "clear light of the reality outside the body"[21] or the "Ground Luminosity,"[22] which is like the light of the day. It has to do with the six-fold knot near the hart chakra. If this knot unwinds, our very subtle consciousness will leave its location and is driven by our evolutionary motivation, our karma, into our next identity. It is obviously the most critical moment of dying, and the unwinding of the knot should preferably be done in a controlled manner. This requires great study and preparation during life because it is in this stage where we can exert our influence over the momentum of our evolution. It is the stage of the highest transparency, without duality (without the notions of "me" and the "others"), without time or eternity, without subject or object, without anything.

Most of us, however, will not have the faintest idea about these eight stages and the existence of this knot, and therefore it will unravel itself suddenly. We will have little control over it and no influence over what happens after it. The clear light stage will pass quickly and before we know it we will find ourselves in front of the entrance of a womb. From this eighth stage, we'll then follow the seven other stages again, but in reverse order: the black stage, the red drop, the white drop and the four elements.[23] And pop!—we are in a new life form, and it is not necessarily a human form. It so happens that we can chose from six different life forms, each leading to reincarnation.

THE BLACK STAGE AND THAT CLEAR-LIGHT STAGE

The first six stages, in which there is description of the dissolving of the four elements and the male and female cognition drops, I cannot place in the context of an NDE. But for the last two stages I clearly can. The seventh stage is described as a blackness, like an empty sky shrouded in utter darkness. This can be compared with what NDEers describe when they are in a dark tunnel, or in a cave, or just in a dark area. They don't see anything, although sometimes they hear a sharp sound, like rattling or whistling, but in any case it is completely dark. Usually they don't experience this darkness as unpleasant. On the contrary, it feels nice and safe.

Then there is the eighth stage of the clear light of the reality outside the body. That has also been translated as the stage of the ground light (something like a back and foreground light). It is the stage in which there is an open sky without mist or clouds. We dwell in a huge openness of light that is like the light of the day or daybreak. Indeed, in NDEs a light often appears. First we think of the all-embracing Light that is full of love and forgiveness because when this Light is seen, it makes a profound and lasting impression on people. It radiates an unearthly and all-embracing love and warmth that cannot be described in words. However, in NDEs light also appears in many other ways. It appears at the end of the tunnel as a small speck that grows and grows and which eventually is all around us. It also happens, for instance, when NDEers see light coming from the trees around them on the spot where they nearly "died." Sometimes they also see beings of light or deceased family members who are veiled in light, and also they may see parks, landscapes, and buildings filled with light. In this way *The Book of the Dead* seems to match what is seen in NDEs: light seems to be the "base color" that is all around when we are dead.

A CONSCIOUSNESS IN THE INTERMEDIATE STATE

The Tibetan Book of the Dead assumes that the consciousness can exist outside the body. The consciousness is then in the intermediate state, and when it is in that state it can continue thinking, hearing, and seeing. An independent consciousness also seems to occur in NDEs. People who, for example, leave their body as a result of an accident, can still see the living. They see how doctors and nurses help them; they see how people around them react, and they see the surrounding area where it all happens. They also hear everything. They hear how the doctors give instructions and they hear the medical equipment. They hear how family members panic or cry. According to blind NDEers they can somehow also feel the surroundings. They are all capable of thinking. What they cannot do, however, is communicate with the non-deceased on Earth. That seems to be impossible. However much NDEers try, they cannot contact us. The communication is one-sided. And exactly that is where *The Tibetan Book of the Dead* starts.

The starting point of *The Tibetan Book of the Dead* is that the living read it to the recently deceased. And they can continue reading for quite a while because the deceased could wander around till forty-nine days after death. The deceased seem to do that in an imaginary world, because in several parts of the Tibetan book it is mentioned that they will have strange visions. It is all, so to speak, "in our own head" when we have these visions. It all comes from our own thoughts. But the visions form a reality outside the body.

So far this resembles NDEs a lot. But there is also a lot that doesn't resemble NDEs. *The Tibetan Book of the Dead* gives the impression that there are very many unpleasant and fearful visions. In reality, however, the number of positive experiences is higher than the number of distressed ones, although we have to consider the possibility that distressful experiences are more quickly forgotten or are not reported to researchers out of shame.

Other things that do not resemble NDEs are the very detailed descriptions in *The Tibetan Book of the Dead*. In NDEs heavenly creatures (either buddhas or other creatures) that sit on lion thrones or other thrones do not occur. In NDEs there are descriptions of beings of light, deceased relatives or other people, but no description of angels with jewels made of human bone, with drums made of human skulls and banners of human skin. There are also no blood-drinking creatures and lords of the death with dog's teeth.

This all may resemble the hell-like visions that are also described in some NDEs. But the impression the book gives is that everyone will have these visions. This is not the case at all for near-death experiences. On the contrary, most NDEs are very pleasant.

What is interesting in *The Tibetan Book of the Dead* is that it repeatedly mentions that the gruesome visions are not real. No one can hit us there because we don't have a body to feel pain, and no one can kill us because we are already dead. The visions come from our own imagination, from our greed, hate, and ignorance.

Finally, The Light is clearly more positively described in NDEs than in *The Tibetan Book of the Dead*. In the book there are different kinds of lights. The clear light is good. The soft light is bad because it will lead you back to one of the six worlds of existence. In NDEs a positive feeling is always attached to light. It is often described as blazing, which could correspond to the clear light of the buddha families. But it is also described as soft and as not hurtful. Either blazing or soft, in NDEs The Light always remains positive.

The Tibetan writer and master Sogyal Rinpoche, who knows about NDEs, also notices the similarities and differences with NDEs. He of course welcomes the similarities. He explains the differences by stressing that NDEs are not true death experiences. The people who have had them came back again. Therefore, they have not had a full experience. The full experience is described in *The Tibetan Book of the Dead*. He also presents the differences for comment to his teacher, who acknowledges that people with an NDE possibly saw something, but also states that their experience still took place in the stage of life. The consciousness leaves the body for a short while for a temporary walk in some of the realms of the afterlife. It may have seen a glimpse of ground light, but not more than that.

This is impossible to oppose. Indeed, it is the case that NDEers all came back again and, therefore, haven't had a full experience. Consequently, it is possible that in a later stage, which no NDEer has gone through, the heavenly creatures on animal thrones will loom and also the angels with jewels made of human bone and all those other descriptions will occur. However, it is impossible to prove or to reject. I suppose it is the advantage of religion that it doesn't have to prove anything. I am yet inclined to regard some of the differences as essential. Some of them I will discuss now.

THE COUNTING OF THE GOOD AND BAD DEEDS

If we didn't take the right turn into nirvana, we have to go back to one of the six worlds of existence. Sinners will get negative visions and good people nice ones.

An essential difference between *The Tibetan Book of the Dead* and the NDEs is the mention of an angel who counts our good deeds and a demon who does the same with our bad deeds. Another essential difference is that we are told that we shouldn't dispute the judgment and if we do, we'll be severely punished.

Nothing in NDEs indicates that another being counts our good and bad deeds. What does happen is that in a number of cases there is a life review, in which we see and feel what the effect of our deeds was on others. This usually happens in the presence of the all-embracing Light that watches lovingly and is full of forgiveness, even when we're of the opinion that we haven't done things right or even may have done things absolutely wrong. The Light leaves the judgment completely up to us and doesn't get angry at any time.

No other than ourselves keeps score. So if the angel and the demon are to be seen as individuals outside of ourselves, then there is a clear difference with NDEs. Of course you can say that the angel and the demon are our own good and bad consciousness. That is also how Francesca Fremantle and Chögyam Trungpa have inter-preted it in their translation of *The Tibetan Book of the Dead*. In that case it is we who, after all, keep score and it seems that the book is right in this matter.

Let's look at the second essential difference. In both translations it is stated that we might dispute the judgment. We will lie and say that we haven't been bad. But the lord of death will look in the mirror of our karma and point at our lies. Then he will become angry and punish us, and it seems that the writer of *The Tibetan Book of the Dead* loved to picture terrible scenes. He will tie a rope around our neck and carry us away, chop off our head, rip out our heart from our body, pull out our intestines, lap up our brains, drink our blood, eat our flesh and chew our bones. But since we are already dead, we will recover so that the torment can start over again from the beginning.

That is an essential difference with NDEs. We judge ourselves, so the instruction that we shouldn't dispute the judgment seems rather strange. It so happens that The Light or another attendant being of light asks questions and occasionally it is said that through these questions we become conscious of the truth. There are the directing questions, but eventually it is we who make our own judgment. In the end there is consensus, so there is nothing left to dispute. Moreover, I do not know of any account in which The Light becomes angry, let alone that it does the terrible things described in The Tibetan Book of the Dead. In all cases The Light remains forgiving.

The tenor of *The Tibetan Book of the Dead* (in the literal transla-tions and not in the interpretations of, for example, Sogyal Rinpoche) is terrifying and negative, while in reality the majority of NDEs are liberating and positive.

The Essence of Buddhism

Buddha is quite silent about the existence of god or God. He seems to think it is not an interesting topic. Yet in Buddhism there is a world of the gods. It is one of the six different worlds of existence, where creatures exist who feel they have an identity. Another one of these six worlds is the one we live in; it is the world of human beings. All the creatures in any of the six worlds, including the gods, are subject to the cycle of life: being alive, dying, and being born again.

The world and our position in it depend on our karma. Karma is like a list of all our actions. They leave an imprint on our most subtle spirit and these imprints will always be there unless they are neutralized. They will come out when we are dead. Then they will materialize, although perhaps not all at once. The actions will determine our future life: the world in which we will be born again and the circumstances we will be in. Therefore, it is very important for everyone to create good actions. These will make it more probable that we will be born in good circumstances.

The idea, however, is that we should not be preoccupied too much with our next life because in each future life there will be suffering. We should try to end the cycle of lives all together, and according to Buddhists escape from this cycle is possible. This is possible when we really understand that our identity is an illusion. We have to acquire this wisdom ourselves. That is what Buddha did without any help from others. And that is what he advises everyone to do. He tells us to trust only ourselves. Nevertheless, he gave us some directions how to do it.

The directions are found in the eightfold path. Important aspects are meditation and the right ethics that have to do with displaying real compassion with all living creatures. The ones who are in the best position to practice compassion are not the gods, the animals, or one of the creatures of one of the other worlds. They are the human beings. We have the best chance to escape from the cycle of life.

Compassion is the magic word. It has to do with feeling real pity for people who are in a less advantageous position, but it also has to do, for instance, with the real joy we should feel for people who have gained something we wanted to accomplish ourselves. In this sense Buddhism is not really different from other religions. All religions in fact preach that we should be good to others. However, Buddhism adds something essential. It adds that the real goal should be that we feel neutral. There should be equanimity on our part. If that is the case we really will have discarded our identity, our "self," and we will be enlightened and enter into nirvana.

Although it sounds very promising that human beings are in the best position to escape the cycle of life, the chances of becoming a human again in next life are very small. And if we are lucky enough to become human again after our death, we still have a long way to go before we can be enlightened. Only a few have reached it. For this reason Buddhism seems to me to be a quite discouraging religion.

Fortunately there is also a ray of hope. It is believed that there are a lot of people who have almost reached the final goal, but who postpone their entrance into nirvana to help others. These people, the bodhisattvas, can keep control over the phase after their death and are able to get back again in a human form to help others find their way.

Foolish Fixations

Just like in all other religions Buddhism has also had its foolish fixations where Buddhists, and even Buddhist monks, interpreted essential basic principles of their beliefs in such a way that they got further away from the essence.

One of the items of the eightfold path prescribes that Buddhists should refrain from harming any living creature. Usually this means that one should refrain from killing humans or animals because it leads to bad karma. Yet in history there are many cases in which Buddhists killed people, even on a massive scale. The most well-known example of course is emperor Ashoka, who must have adhered to Buddhism before his battle and only understood the essence of it after he viewed the battle field.

Some Buddhists have used their religion to gloss over the killing of people. That happened for instance when the Chinese emperor Wen (581–604) waged his wars to unite the country.[24] He had temples built for Buddhist monks on places where he had won his battles. In exchange the monks had to hold memorial services for his fallen soldiers. In that case the still-living soldiers would know that after their possible death there would be active praying for their spiritual welfare. In a way the Buddhist monks compromised themselves with the emperor. When they really wanted to follow the eightfold path, they shouldn't have lent themselves for this purpose, but should have made clear to the emperor that what he was doing was wrong.

A much clearer and also more recent example of Buddhists contributing actively to warfare is what occurred in Japan in the Second World War. Apart from collectively ignoring the eightfold path, the objective of Buddhism (the discarding of the "self") was also actively deployed to support the war activities. The four noble truths prescribe that by following the eightfold path we will learn to understand that there is no difference between "me" and "the others," and that we have to discard the "self" to reach enlightenment.

Buddhist and Zen leaders used this doctrine to arouse a certain state of mind within soldiers and, at the end of the war, also within the whole of the Japanese population. They convinced them that their own life was unimportant. This has been well documented in the books of Brian Daizen Victoria, who concludes that the religious leaders were "thoroughly and completely morally bankrupt."[25] The religious leaders actively made people believe that when the "self" is successfully discarded, life is not important either. The consequence was that for Japanese soldiers and later for the whole Japanese population it became easier to prefer death over life. That idea pervaded the Japanese manual for the soldier (the Field Service Code): "Faith is power; he who has faith and fights resolutely will always be victorious."[26]

When Japan at the start of its expansion in Asia was still strong, this attitude had already led to brutal violations of humanity. The way the Japanese went on a rampage in China for instance, can only be explained by the low value they attached to their own lives and, therefore, also to the lives of others. Those lives were plainly despised.

The "Rape of Nanking" (the city that was capital of China for a long time) is an example of this. It took place in 1937 and ranks as one of the worst atrocities of the war. After the Japanese had taken the city, they butchered an estimated 300,000 people in a horrible way. Many women were raped, some repeatedly ("we took turns raping them"[27]), and the imperial navy on the Yangtze River attacked people fleeing in anything that could float. In the city the captured people were at first decapitated one by one, while the still-to-be decapitated prisoners had to dump the corpses of their predecessors in the river. But that, in the opinion of the Japanese, took too long and they then started to use machine guns.

When my life is not important, then that of my enemy is even less important. Starting from this idea it is no surprise that when expressed in percentages, the number of surviving prisoners of war of the Japanese was much smaller than of the Germans and Italians (73% versus 96%).[28]

The religious subordination of the "self" to the Japanese nationalistic ideal and to the emperor has led to more extreme and foolish fixations. When at the end of the war the awareness of a lost war grew within the Japanese leaders, "Special Attack Forces" were established in 1944. These were military units that performed kamikaze attacks. Kamikaze pilots crashed their planes and themselves into Allied ships. An important point is that they received their training and instructions in Zen temples.

The Buddhist and Zen leaders have also contributed to the acceptance in Japan of the suicide tactic. For instance, in Buddhist papers these attacks were cheered and it was indicated that "the source of the spirit of the Special Attack Forces lies in the denial of the individual self."[29] They made people believe that if they discarded the "self" and fell on the battlefield shouting, "May the emperor live for ten thousand years!" they would be born again in Japan. That alleviated the pain for parents who lost their children in the war. It meant that every new baby could be their son who was killed in battle. General Tojo Hideki, the prime minister and one of the most powerful men in Japan between 1941 and 1944, also wanted of course to be born again in Japan, and for that reason he probably shouted the wish to the emperor just before he was hanged in 1948 for his war crimes.

When the war really seemed to be lost, it was quite explicitly expected from the Japanese civil population that they would act like the military and adhere to the manual for the soldiers. They were supposed to choose death rather than life. On a number of Japanese islands when Americans went ashore after long battles, this led to a lot of suicides within the civilian population. An American described it as follows: "In a carnival of death that shocked even battle-hardened Marines, whole families waded into the sea to drown together or huddled together to blow themselves up with grenades; parents tossed their children off cliffs before leaping to join them in death."[30]

This is what can happen when essential basic religious principles are interpreted in a way to suit a certain group or cause. It reminds us of the way in which some Muslims gloss over their suicide commandos.

$\backsim$ 5 $\backsim$

Judaism

I AM WHO I AM

The Establishing of Monotheism[1]

Judaism is probably not a "world" religion since it is practiced by a limited number of people. According to estimates, the Jewish religion includes just about 15 million people worldwide.[2] However, the most striking thing about Judaism is that it is the basis for two other religions that are practiced by many more people. Those two religions are Christianity (started in the first century of the Western calendar) and Islam (started in 622 of the Western calendar). Christianity is assumed to have about 2 billion member-believers, while the number of Muslims, which has been growing rapidly for years, already exceeds 1.2 billion. It is because of these reasons that a separate chapter is dedicated to Judaism.

Both of the derived religions attach great importance to the Jewish scriptures, mainly to the Tanakh, the Jewish Bible. Christians have adopted the Tanakh in its entirety, even though they have made changes to the order of the books. The result is known as the "Old Testament." Mohammed doesn't go that far, but often refers to the stories in the Tanakh, and says that the Jewish scriptures are taken from a "primal book" from which also Christ and he were reciting.

There are two groups of stories that connect the three religions the most. In the first place there are the stories about the creation of the world and the creation of the first humans, Adam and Eve. In the second place there are the stories revolving around the patriarch Abraham, who is recognized by the three religions as the common basis for their respective beliefs. The reason is that Abraham was the first man to introduce monotheism. That was an innovation because at that time it was common practice to have several gods who were attached, for instance, to a natural phenomenon (e.g., fire, water, sun) or a location (e.g., a tree, a rock, the sea).

According to monotheism there is only one God, who is so general that he is not attached to anything, nor bound by anything. That is why in the Jewish monotheism the name of God is: "I am who I am." A more general reference to God is almost unthinkable. Moreover, this name is so holy that it may not be pronounced in full. That is why it is abbreviated and, according to the Jewish writing, it is YHWH.

Along with the story of the Creation and the stories about Abraham there is another story that, particularly in the Jewish religion, has great importance. It is the exodus from Egypt led by Moses. The importance of this story lies in the subsequent specification of Judaism by Moses who passed on the revelations of YHWH to the Jewish people. These revelations are comprised in five books that together are called the "Torah," which forms a part of the Tanakh. All that is in the Tanakh is considered a revelation, but especially important are the parts of the Torah containing the Ten Commandments, the many dietary laws, and the holy assignment to the Jewish people. That is why Moses is seen by the Jews as the greatest prophet and can be compared in importance with Christ for the Christians and Mohammed for the Muslims.

The Sacred Texts

The books of Moses are not one text. They are a compilation of many different documents from different periods. The period, in which the books were written extends from 850 BC to 450 BC. Although the Bible at first glance seems to be one continuous story, on further consideration that is not the case. In general, it is scientifically accepted that the Bible derives from several sources.[3] One can also recognize several turns of phrase in the writings. At some point in time all the different sources were put in order and combined into one whole. Sometimes several stories that resembled each other were put in succession, like the two stories of the Creation (see next subsection). Sometimes cut and pasting has mixed the texts up.

A lot of what is written in the Torah is there to encourage us to love our neighbor as ourselves.[4] This golden rule clearly indicates that love for our fellow man is one of the most important things in life. The addition "as ourselves" has more meaning than we would think at first glance. It shows that the other is just as important as we are. And it also shows that we are important too. When, for instance, we are in a "dip" or even in a real depression and we cannot really find ways to love ourselves, we would also be excused, to some extent, from loving others. Apparently there is the understanding that in that situation we do not have enough energy to love others. But when we are standing on top of the world and feel as if we are the greatest of all, then we are required to love others in a similar way.

LOVE YOURSELF

It may sound strange, but we have to love ourselves. This is made very clear in the example of the NDEer who lived in the dysfunctional family (as I discussed in chapter 2 in subsection "Everyone is important").[5] The reason behind this is that everyone has a divine spark within him- or herself. If we don't have respect for ourselves, it in fact means that we don't have respect for that part of God within ourselves, or for the part of God that we are.

In our busy world focused on success and performance, it regularly occurs that people end up in a tight corner. That can take all sorts of forms. It begins early at school where children tease each other and some children are victims of that teasing more often than others. Teasing and intimidation can also take place within the family, or in the working environment, or anywhere. In order to gain their own position in society, some people feel the need to demean others and to misuse them physically or emotionally. Some people do it because they haven't had a good role model in their youth and don't understand that they hurt others with their conduct. In all cases the behavior of the one who inflicts the indignities is far from optimal, but, surprisingly, neither is it optimal when the victim allows these indignities to happen.

We shouldn't let others misuse us; we shouldn't let ourselves be intimidated or teased. If we do that, we in fact do not have respect for the God within us. Moreover, there is no reason to see ourselves as less than others, and we should certainly not see ourselves as less than the one who is abusing or intimidating us. There are no "lesser" souls. The hierarchy in the unseen part of Unity Universe is totally different from the visible part on earth. It is not comparable. The Light thinks everybody is important and valuable.

I have to stress, incidentally, that Judaism does not believe that we all have a part of God within us like Hinduism does. On the contrary, according to Judaism, YHWH is an entity outside us. Nevertheless, we have to love ourselves as we love others. This implies that we shouldn't degrade ourselves or respect ourselves less.

The question is how we can do that in a situation in which we are physically or emotionally abused or intimidated and from which it seems to be impossible to escape. One can find enough people who are in a hopeless situation. The answer of the NDEer is that there would always be several honorable alternatives in which quiet and peace are possible. They are sometimes difficult to realize, but they are there. And when we actually realize one of these alternatives, it brings spiritual growth for all parties involved. This NDEer was allowed to see how much growth eventually took place in people's lives when they finally overcame their "background" and had a reaction with love and compassion instead of a reaction with the purpose to cause pain or aggression. She also saw how love and compassion from non-involved parties could facilitate positive changes in the lives of the involved parties.[6]

Another important passage in the Torah is:[7] "Hear, O Israel, the Lord our God is one Lord. And you shall love the Lord your God with all your heart, and with all your soul, and with all your might."

This pronouncement given by Moses is seen by the Jews as one of the most important sections in the scriptures. It is their profession of faith. This commandment and the commandment to love others as yourself are repeated by Jesus and joined together when he is asked what is the most important commandment (see in next chapter "The Teachings of Jesus").[8]

In Jewish history the people were regularly suppressed, persecuted, or even deported in their entirety. Important examples mentioned in the Jewish Bible are the periods of enslavement in Egypt (possibly during the beginning of the 20th dynasty around 1300 BC) and Babylonia (after the destruction of Jerusalem by King Nebuchadnezzar in 587 BC). Of course, not mentioned in the Bible are the suppression during the Roman occupation and the Holocaust in Europe at the time of World War II.

What the Holocaust is generally known and understandably remembered for, is the most awful example of what hate can cause. But what the Romans did at the beginning of the Christian Era was just as terrible. After an uprising, the big temple in Jerusalem, so tremendously important to the Jews, was torn down by the Romans in the year AD 70. The shock of that destruction could be compared to the shock that would be felt by the destruction of Saint Peter's Basilica in Rome or the Ka'bah in Mecca.

At the entrance of the Forum in Rome there is still a triumphal arch in honor of Titus, the man who was responsible for the fires that destroyed the Second Temple of Jerusalem when his army invaded the city. According to the Roman historian Josephus, Titus did not originally intend to destroy the Second Temple when he entered Jerusalem, but the furious Roman soldiers did. During the siege and subsequent sack of Jerusalem as many as 1,100,000 people perished, mainly Jews, and almost 100,000 were enslaved. After this battle and siege the city ceased to be Jewish for the next two thousand years. Historian Josephus also reports about the entry of Titus in the Forum with cartloads of artifacts: "The most interesting of all were the spoils seized from the Temple of Jerusalem. ... The law of the Jews (author: perhaps these were the tablets of the Law of Moses?) was borne along after these as the last of the spoils." Then the Jewish slaves followed, and finally the triumphant Titus who became emperor of the Roman Empire in AD 79 and reigned until his death two years later in 81. All of this can still be seen, since it is depicted on the inside of his triumphal arch in Rome.

The occupation of Jerusalem continued and so did the resistance against it. During the reign of Emperor Hadrian it came to a crisis. After an uprising in AD 132 the Romans had had enough. The Jews were banned from Jerusalem and the number of Jews in the area fell sharply. This is regarded as the start of the Diaspora, the dispersion of the Jewish people into the then known world. During this time the Talmud was composed, which comprised the regulations and teachings from the Tanakh as well as the practical rules that were developed over the course of time. There are many rules, too many to fathom: 613! From these there are 248 dos and 365 don'ts. The purpose of this overdose of prescriptions and rules is to reach some uniformity in the Jewish belief, despite the distances over which the Jews were dispersed. They are also aimed at changing the individual, and by doing so also at changing society. Jews also point out that the many do's and don'ts are not meant by YHWH as an absurd burden on the Jews. Instead, they say that when they live strictly by these rules, they show their submission to YHWH.

THE FORMAL SIDES OF A RELIGION

The 613 do's and don'ts are quite intriguing. Why do they exist? What is their purpose? It seems that many of them had originally been very useful. Some thousands of years ago, eating of pork was very unhealthy because of the possible contamination with parasites. The institution of a year of rest for the cultivation of a piece of land (six years of cultivation, and to avoid exhaustion of the land one year of rest was required) was very good for the agricultural production in the long run. The prohibition to have intercourse with, for instance, your sister, your aunt or any other close family member was very useful to avoid inbreeding. Unfortunately this prohibition didn't go far enough, because cousins were allowed to marry, which in the Arabic countries (where these rules were adopted by Mohammed) led to a whole range of physical defects.

But apart from these meaningful do's and don'ts there are a number that do not seem to be meaningful and, therefore, raise big questions. For instance, Jews are not allowed to eat the hip muscle because an angel (or YHWH himself, which is a little unclear) kicked the hip muscle of Jacob during a fight.

Are we allowed to be more critical of religious do's and don'ts? According to NDEers true spirituality is not about rules and about strictly following them. It doesn't revolve around the formal sides of religions. It should not be about what one should and shouldn't eat, how often we should kneel, how we should dress, which days we are supposed not to work, and so forth). Important is the essence of religions, not its form.

Every true spiritual way leads to The Light. A religion can be helpful to find true spirituality, but the formal sides of a religion may very well obscure this. Many examples can be found at the end of each chapter, in the sections on "Foolish fixations." Moreover, rules and regulations create boundaries, whereas The Light doesn't draw boundaries. An NDEer told me that God is freedom: "*We pose restrictions on ourselves. We make prisons in our own head. We even allow others to make prisons in our own head by accepting the restrictions they pose upon us.*"

This NDEer and many others have discovered something else during their experience, something that they say is far more important that the formal sides of any religion. They understand that life is not about strictly adhering to any rule, but about love for other people and nature. It is especially about the general kind of love, which is love that is not aimed at one or a few persons, but at everyone, as if everyone is equal. And love can also be aimed at animals and at nature in general. It is about love in the broadest sense. It is about how we have shown that love. How did we react to others and to nature? Was it with love, or was it with anger and destruction? Was it with tolerance or intolerance? And what was our true inner intention?

In the "Begin Situation"

The Jewish Bible, and therefore also the Christian Bible, begin with the creation of the world by YHWH. The story is in the first book and starts with the words: "In the begin situation God created the heaven and the earth." Consequently, the name of the book is "In the begin situation" or "In the beginning," which in Hebrew is "B'reshit" and in Latin "Genesis."[9]

The story of the creation is a peculiar story; it takes place at high speed, namely in six days. In succession were created: the light, the heaven, the earth, the sea and the green plants, the sun, moon and the stars, the fish, the birds, and the other animals and at last also human beings, both man and woman. The first man (or protohuman) is made from clay and comes to life after YHWH blows his breath into it. He has no name, but is simply called (proto)human, which in Hebrew is "Adam." What is special about the creation of Adam is that he is created "in YHWH's own image." What that means seems to be the same in both the derived religions and perhaps also in Judaism: God is always seen as a male. It is also interesting that the clay comes to life after YHWH blows the spirit into it.[10]

THE SIXTH DAY YHWH BREATHES LIFE INTO MAN

Man is brought to life by the breath of God. His breath, therefore, is in everyone who lives. Because He breathed his breath into us, we come to life.

During her experience an NDEer asks what The Light is. The answer was very interesting. She was told that The Light is not God, but it is when God breathes. Therefore, The Light is in everyone and that is in effect also what is often said by NDEers: we are all parts of God, we all have The Light in us and for that reason we all deserve respect.

It is remarkable that in the first chapter of the book B'reshit man is created last, while in the second chapter man is created before the animals and the birds. From this it is clear that there are in fact two stories of the Creation that are placed one after another. And that means that there should be at least two different authors.

At first, when the (proto)human and the female human are together, everything goes well. She doesn't have a name yet and is referred to as female human. It is like a fairy tale; they are very happy together. This ends when the snake throws in a wrench. That happens when he persuades the female human to go against YHWH's orders and eat from the fruit of the "Tree of the Knowing of Good and Evil." According to the snake they would become just like YHWH and have the knowledge about good and evil. After the female human, the (proto)human also eats the forbidden fruit (by the way: an apple is mentioned nowhere) and with that the Fall of Men becomes a fact.

The consequences are terrible. YHWH becomes very angry and gives out several punishments to them. For the woman He makes pregnancy more arduous (with pains shall you bear children, but nevertheless the woman shall continue to lust for a man) and He lets the man rule her. Since the female human will have to bear children, Adam calls her Havva, which means Eve, the giver of life. The punishment for man is that he will have to toil for food. Moreover, both humans will return to dust. In other words: they will die. In the Christian tradition this is the most important effect of the Fall and for neutralizing this, Christ has to come into the world (see next chapter).

Meanwhile Adam and Eve have discovered that they are naked and they are ashamed of it. They take some leaves to cover themselves. Despite his anger, YHWH is very caring and makes clothes for Adam and Eve. After that He nevertheless chases them out of paradise. He has a good reason for it. Now that both humans have knowledge of good and evil and have almost become like YHWH, He wants to avoid them becoming fully like Him. In paradise there is another tree, the tree of life. Eating the fruit of this tree would mean that humans would also become immortal, and then they would have the two most important divine characteristics. To prevent them from finding this tree, winged sphinxes with flaming swords guard the way. In fact these are supernatural creatures. In Hebrew it says "cherubim," which is often translated as cherubs and which in the West has been changed into "angels," and even into small, bloated, baby angels, which can often be seen in paintings.

According to Judaism, an important consequence of the expulsion from paradise is that humans have to continue working on the Creation. It so happens that in the Torah "Creation" is seen as incomplete. Man is needed to work on it. And since man is created in YHWH's own image, he has to create just like YHWH. That is his task.[11]

OUR TASK IS TO CONTINUE WORKING ON CREATION

The moral sense is the most important difference between humans and the other animals. How did it happen that we, as monkeys, changed into humans with a moral sense? Something seems to be written about this in B'reshit/Genesis: moral sense has come over us after eating from the tree with that peculiar name, the Tree of the Knowing of Good and Evil.

The difference between man and animal is also that we use clothes. After eating from the forbidden fruit the two humans want to dress themselves immediately. The story of the Fall of Man seems therefore nothing else than a simplified account of the essential transformation from animal (proto)human into a human with moral concepts.

What is interesting is that according to Judaism the development of man did not stop after this transformation. It now is our task to continue to work on creation. YHWH has created the correct environment for us and after six days He rests. And while He does that, it is our task to continue his work. But what is it we have to do?

Creation has shown two sides: a material side (from a ball of gas to an earth with green grasslands and cows on it) and a spiritual side (from animals without moral sense to those with moral sense). We possibly have to work on both fronts. That also seems to be manifest in some of the NDEs. While we are on Earth, we all have a task to complete. What that task is, is often not clear, but from some accounts one can conclude that this task is very individual. From other accounts it seems that the task can also be performed together with others. It can be a materialistic task, and remember that nature is considered as a very important and valuable material. The task can also be spiritual. In any case, from the many NDEs it seems that life is just one intermediate phase in a very great work, of which we all are part and in which we all have to contribute somehow.

The Covenants with YHWH

After Adam and Eve some other descendants are mentioned in B'reshit/ Genesis. An important descendant is Noah, who had to deal with the Flood, the big flooding in which the whole earth is supposed to have drowned. The sign of peace, the dove with an olive branch, originates from this story.

Following directions from YHWH, Noah made a boat, in which he gathered all animals, two of each kind. Since the other people were disobedient towards YHWH, He let it rain firmly for forty days and forty nights, so that all those disobedient people drowned. Only Noah, his sons, his wife, and the wives of his sons remained (apparently he had no daughters, or they drowned too). Because he had to bring two of each kind of animal, creation could restore itself again after the disaster.

After the rainfall and the flooding, the water subsided again. To see if there was enough dry land, he let a dove go free. The second time he did this the dove came back with a fresh olive leaf in its beak. Noah concluded that everything had returned to its normal proportion again. Since YHWH thought that it had been a little bit too harsh to exterminate all living creatures, He made a covenant with Noah, his sons, their descendants, and with all living creatures on earth. The promise YHWH made is that He would never let a flood destroy the earth again. What He said was: "I will never curse the soil again on humankind's account, since what the human heart forms, is evil from its youth."[12] He promised never to interfere in the natural processes, because "as long as the earth exists, seedtime and harvest, cold and heat, summer and winter, day and night shall not cease." He presented the rainbow as the sign of that promise.

However, man had to set himself the task of doing something too. He had to multiply. To make that possible sufficient food was required and YHWH allowed man to eat all things that were crawling about and also the green plants. Nevertheless, man had to respect the sanctity of the life of animals. Animals could be killed for food, but the life had to be out of the flesh. Blood is thought to be life, and that is why Jews definitely may not consume blood (meat has to be bloodless).

Man could eat all things that crawl about. All? To make sure that Noah and his descendants would not think of using other people as food, it was explicitly prohibited to kill other people. The resolute shedding of human blood is even penalized with death: "Whoever sheds human blood, for that human his blood shall be shed."[13]

In this first covenant justice is introduced. Two more covenants between YHWH and the humans followed. The second covenant is with Abraham, the patriarch, who is also acknowledged by Christians and Muslims. In that covenant righteousness is introduced. The third covenant is with Moses and in it "Israel" is appointed by YHWH as "a kingdom of priests" that should serve humanity.[14]

DON'T KILL PEOPLE, INCLUDING YOURSELF

In the first covenant YHWH promises never to intervene in nature to destroy people. He sees that the "evil" of people is due to their primitiveness (youth) and for that reason He desires that they multiply and consequently develop themselves. For that purpose they are allowed to expand their diet. Man doesn't have to restrict himself to the consumption of only vegetables, but may now also consume meat. What is interesting is that it is explicitly demanded that the life has to be out of the flesh.

Apparently animals have a valuable life too, which should be dealt with respectfully. The killing of people is strictly forbidden. From NDEs it is always apparent that the killing of people (also of ourselves) is one of the worst things to do. The reason seems to be that we deprive someone of the possibility to fulfill his task and thus to finish his or her development. Life is seen as a tremendous gift, which is given to us for our own individual development and with which we can also contribute a bit to the collective development of us all together. NDEers say that by committing suicide, we throw back the gift of life to the one who gave it to us (YHWH or The Light), so that we abruptly stop our own development. Something similar also applies to murder. By committing murder, we take away the gift of life given to someone else. It is just as bad as suicide.

With respect to the end of man and animals YHWH promises that He will not bring that about. But we can do it ourselves. We don't need YHWH for that. We just have to see how we exhaust natural resources and how we change the balance of the eco system and heat the earth up. Maybe that is just as bad as committing suicide (or murder): we maltreat another gift, namely nature.

Abraham: The Second Covenant and a Numerous People

Abram, as Abraham is initially called, is head of a family of nomads.[15] From YHWH he hears that he has to go to the country that YHWH will show him and where Abram will create a large people, just as numerous as the stars in the sky[16] or as the dust of the earth.[17]

Contrary to his father, Abram is an "ethical monotheist," which means that his God is not bound by an area or a phenomenon of nature, like the moon, the sun, or the thunder. He is the Creator of all areas and of all phenomena of nature. Moreover, that One God is an ethical God, who takes an interest in justice and righteousness. All of this is central to Abram's belief, together with the belief in one God. How Abram independently came to such a belief remains a mystery.[18]

When Abram arrives at a specific crossroads of trade routes, YHWH appears in a revelation and promises this land to him and his offspring.[19] At that moment he is in Canaan, an area just north of Jerusalem. However, there is a problem: His wife Sarai proves not to be able to get children. Having children is quite essential to be able to produce numerous offspring. She persuades Abram to beget a child with her Egyptian slave.[20] Abram does that. But then a period of envy between the two women follows. The slave Hagar looks down on Sarai because she can't have a child and, in return, Sarai becomes jealous. She regrets her recommendation to Abram and goes to him to talk about it. Interestingly, this demonstrates the equality between the patriarch and his wife.

Abram thinks everything is quite simple. He points out to Sarai that strictly speaking Hagar is her slave and she can do with her slave whatever she wants. Hagar senses the lack of support from Abram and becomes afraid. She flees into the desert and whimpers about her humiliation by Sarai. Eventually, an angel orders her to go back and to undergo the harassments of Sarai.[21] The angel promises her that her offspring will be so numerous that they will be uncountable. Later the child is born and is named Ishmael, which means "YHWH will hear" or "YHWH had heard" her whimpering. Abram by then had attained the improbably high age of 86 years.

Ishmael is a very important person because Muslims see him as the one they descended from. As far as that is concerned, the promise of the angel was right, because at this moment the followers of Mohammed are almost just as numerous as the number of Christians.

Thirteen years after the birth of Ishmael YHWH makes a covenant with Abram. YHWH promises that Abram will become patriarch of numerous offspring. "Kings shall come out of you." The name of Abram is changed into Abraham, which means "father of many nations." Sarai's name is changed too. It becomes Sarah, or "queen." Moreover, the land where they are (Canaan) is donated to Abraham to be his eternal property. But all of this doesn't happen for free. Abraham has to do something for it. He and all men of his retinue have to strip themselves of their foreskin. It doesn't only involve family, but also friends and slaves. In this way the covenant of YHWH is visible in their flesh.[22]

YHWH tells Abraham and Sarah that they will have a child, but Abraham really has to laugh about it. They both are older than 90 years! However, the miracle happens and they give birth to Isaac, which means, "He laughs."

The problems between Hagar and Sarah have not disappeared, and now it is Ishmael who provides the fuel. He laughs about Isaac and this

AN UNLIMITED GOD

The family problems of Abraham, which in fact continue to this very day, almost obscure the most important aspect of Abraham: the introduction of the ethical monotheism. God is not bound to a place or a natural phenomenon. God is not that limited; He is much more than that. He is unlimited.

Likewise The Light that one sometimes gets to see at the end of the tunnel in NDEs is not bound to any earthly limitations and is always described as very comprehensive. NDEers have great difficulty finding words to describe The Light and its unconditional love. Of course the question remains whether this Light is the same as YHWH, God, or Allah, but NDEers certainly feel that it is of a higher divine nature.

really annoys Sarah. To secure Isaac's rights she presses Abraham to send Hagar and Ishmael away. Abraham does this after he obtains YHWH's consent. Hagar and her son lose their way in the desert and Ishmael starts crying. YHWH hears the crying (this also fits with his name) and He shows them a well that they can drink from. Ishmael grows up, marries an Egyptian woman, and starts living in what is now known as Saudi Arabia.[23] With this the story of Ishmael in Judaism ends, but for Muslims it continues.

As if two sons were not enough, Abraham had another six children after Sarah died. He had the first of these six when he was 127 years old. Eventually he reaches the age of 175 and is buried by Isaac and Ishmael together.

Moses: The Third Covenant

At one time the wandering Jewish people are stuck in Egypt where they are enslaved. Their liberation comes through Moses, but it isn't without striking a blow.[24] The pharaoh doesn't want to listen to an insignificant guy who just wandered out of the desert into his palace and demands the release of the Israelites. Therefore YHWH sends nine disasters to Egypt. The tenth plague is too much for the pharaoh because YHWH takes the lives of all first-borns, including the oldest son of the pharaoh.

Three months after the flight from Egypt something very important happens. YHWH confirms a covenant with the Israelites and three days after that, in a staging that would even be too much for Hollywood, Moses receives the Ten Commandments. This happens in the desert on Mount Sinai, which is enshrouded in smoke, clouds, fire, thunder, lightning and even the blast of trumpets. And as if that is not enough, there is an earthquake during the time that YHWH is present on the mountain.[25]

In the covenant with the Israelites YHWH states that "You will be to Me a kingdom of priests, and a holy nation."[26] With this covenant YHWH makes the Jews the chosen people with an important task for the world. By following a special way of living placed in the service of YHWH, the people of Israel have to distinguish themselves from other peoples. By doing that, they would serve mankind.[27] The special manner of living is incorporated in a multitude of do's and don'ts. Part of this is the stringent dietary laws.

It is logical that this special position of the Jewish people given to them by YHWH himself has led to considerable jealousy with the two derived religions. Mohammed was at first favorably disposed towards the Jews, but when they didn't hold his revelations as true he became more and more hostile. For instance, he concluded that the many dietary laws were a punishment imposed by Allah on the Jews.

Christians found a totally different argument in order to approach the Jews with hostility. According to them the Jews were foolish enough not to see that Jesus Christ was the long-expected Messiah and they are even to blame for his suffering and death.

The Ten Commandments that were presented with thunder, lightning, and the blast of trumpets formed the central point of the Jewish religion, and the Jews attach a universal meaning to the commandments. There are many interesting aspects of the commandments. One is that the commandments are directed to the individual. The "you" to whom the commandments are addressed is you and not the group. This means that you have a free will, something that many NDEers also say. Another interesting point is that the first four commandments relate to God and the other six to the people amongst themselves. Also, one should note that no real punishments are held out to the prospect when "you" do not observe the commandments. Yet, trespassing is not totally "free." In ancient Israel all offences were seen as offences against YHWH.[28]

The first commandment prohibits having other gods besides YHWH ("I am who I am"). The second commandment describes extensively that it is prohibited to deify nature and that graven images are not allowed because it tarnishes his Being. Worshipping such images makes YHWH jealous. With this the monotheism of Abraham is confirmed: YHWH is independent of area or nature.

The third commandment states that "you" shall not take the name of YHWH in vain. It is explicitly mentioned that YHWH will not accept this. The ban on taking his name in vain is often interpreted as a ban on cursing, in which the word God appears. However, taking his name in vain goes much further than that. When someone says he knows what God's intentions are and uses it to impose his own will on others, he already takes his name in vain. When someone uses God's message for his own profit, he then takes his name in vain. When someone does things in the name of God that hurt another human either physically or mentally, that person is definitely taking his name in vain.[30]

This covers many things, such as waging wars in his name, something which Christians and Muslims are extensively guilty of. It also covers promising, in his name, that a knight who goes on a crusade will go to heaven straight away. Or promising in his name that someone who ignites a bomb in a crowd to "protect Islam" will receive in heaven, as a reward, a large number of "virginal companions." And recently I was amazed by what some American politicians told the public: the 2011 earthquake south of Washington and the hurricane that reached New England a month later were punishments from God for the bad politics in Washington. This is also a trespass against the third commandment. God will not let all of this pass. So, don't do or say anything in his name, unless you are absolutely sure that it has a loving intention.

The fourth commandment states that "you" have to observe the seventh day (the Sabbath day), the day of rest. This day of rest means that no one shall work, not a son or daughter, not a servant, or someone who stays with you temporarily, or not even an animal.

The remaining commandments concern the respect amongst people themselves. It starts in the fifth commandment with the command to have respect for your parents. Then, in the sixth commandment, there must be the respect for life: you shall not kill. This actually is a repeat of what has already been said in the covenant with Noah. In the seventh commandment the respect for your beloved one is brought forward by stating that you shouldn't commit adultery. In the eighth commandment the respect for the possessions of others is given: you are not to steal. The last two commandments can be summarized as an encouragement to avoid each word and thought that can hurt a fellow man. The ninth commandment states that you should not bear false witness against your neighbor. In the tenth commandment it says that you should also be careful with your desires. You shouldn't desire things that belong to your neighbor.

After the Ten Commandments the Israelites could not directly enter the promised land of Canaan. In total they had to cross the Sinai desert for forty years. After that period only Moses was prevented by YHWH to enter the country. In the Jewish text it literally says that Moses dies "by the mouth of YHWH." In the Christian bible it is quite unclear; it is stated that Moses dies "according to the word of YHWH." However, the literal interpretation of the Jewish text gave rise to the Jewish tradition that Moses died by a divine kiss.[29]

A kiss from YHWH to end life is a wonderful thought. Who wouldn't want to end his or her life with such a divine kiss? If you give it a bit of a thought it might actually happen to everyone. Remember that an NDEers said that The Light isn't God, but the breath of God. Then just as YHWH breathed life in us when we were born, will YHWH take his/her breath back again with a kiss. With this we can then return home to where we originated, to YHWH. In this way YHWH will kiss us all.

No Punishments

The commandments are addressed to the individual. Apparently we are individually liable for our deeds. That no explicit punishments are mentioned is remarkable and matches NDEs. Also, there is no mention of punishments imposed by someone else, such as The Light.

From NDEs it can be derived that a possible punishment comes from the individual himself, who is ashamed of the non-optimal choices that he has made. This feeling of shame arises when he is in the warm loving Light, who shows him all the effects of his non-optimal choices. In the presence of the unconditional love of The Light the individual sees his own shortcomings. And when he denies them, there still is no punishment. The Light doesn't punish. I don't know of a single NDE in which The Light becomes angry and imposes a punishment. It will at worst ask questions that will direct the individual to the process of recognition of everything where he or she has failed. For example: "What did you really think, when you did that?"

An NDEer said that we don't even punish ourselves. In fact, the word punishment is wrong. It is more like the feeling of having wasted a good opportunity to choose for a more optimal alternative through which the energy or love in universe could have grown.

An important part of understanding all the effects of our non-optimal choices is reliving the pain it caused others. The feelings of shame someone has after reliving these non-optimal choices are directed at himself and at The Light. And even though The Light, according to the reports, always remains neutral but loving, it seems that the shame arises from the feeling of having "offended" The Light. In that sense one could see the "offences" against YHWH.

MAKE NO REPRESENTATION OF YHWH

The ban on making representations of YHWH is also adopted, in principle, by Christians. However, Roman Catholics in particular have not observed this ban. In many churches one can admire pictures of God as an old man with a grey or white beard and in the Sistine Chapel Michelangelo once even depicted Him with his bottom facing the spectator.

The reason why He is depicted as a man has probably to do with the creation of Adam. He is created in God's own image. However, by picturing God in a human form you could think that He too descends from monkeys, and that doesn't seem correct. It severely tarnishes his Being.

"In His own image" probably refers to the spiritual image, the one that flies through the tunnel after the body has died. Moreover, people who have had an NDE have a lot of problems trying to describe all that they have experienced and especially The Light that they sometimes encountered at the end of the tunnel. That is why it is better to take this second commandment literally and to make no representation of YHWH, not even in your own mind. It will always be inadequate in all respects. For this reason it is absolutely prohibited for Jews and Muslims to make a representation of YHWH or Allah.

GOOD THOUGHTS

The last six commandments all center around having respect for each other. That applies to your parents, to the life of others (and ourselves), to the possessions of others to the feelings of your beloved one(s) and those of anyone else. With the latter it is explicitly stated that you also have to be careful with what you think.

During the life review in NDEs the respect for others is an important theme. And thoughts seem to be of great importance too. Sometimes it is said that one should be careful with one's thoughts because they can materialize. How that works, I don't know, but it is mentioned often by NDEers.

Also it is good when one grants something to other people. To have compassion for someone who is worse off is rather easy. To have compassion for someone who is better off is more difficult, but just as important. It involves being really happy when someone else has something nice, like a good promotion, an expensive car, many sons (in some cultures this seems to be very important), a good lover, and so on.

Job

In the Tanakh many beautiful stories appear and one is about Job. He is a rich man who becomes the victim of the dispute between YHWH and the devil. YHWH wants to prove to the devil that Job will accept all his suffering. He allows the devil to put Job to the test. The devil really pulls all the stops. Job becomes impoverished and loses everything, his wife leaves him, he is covered with ulcers, and his children die when the house collapses in which they had a party. In short, it cannot become worse. He ends on a dunghill. Despite a single outburst of anger Job holds his ground: "We accept good things from YHWH; and should we not accept evil?"[31] Interesting is also a statement of Solomon. He said that since one cannot comprehend the rule of YHWH, one should not concentrate on comprehending it. One should concentrate on living as correct as possible.[32]

WHY DOES THIS HAPPEN TO ME!?

Why is there misfortune in everyone's life? Why does misfortune strike some people more than others? Why are there war, disease, and strife? It seems there is never an answer to all of this. Job's answer is that we have to accept the fortune as well as the misfortune. And Solomon's answer is that we shouldn't understand what the reason for everything is, but that we have to continue to try to do well.

And in a certain way NDEers say this too. Setbacks and misfortune are not bad. They have a purpose, and it is not negative. In any case it isn't there as a punishment. The Light or God does not punish. Neither does The Light or God wants to tease us or to thwart us in any way. On the contrary. According to NDEers there is a good and positive reason for setbacks and misfortune. Unfortunately they fail to clearly explain what that positive reason is.

What they do know is that problems and setbacks create the possibility to make choices and through these choices we are able to demonstrate our love. When there is no conflict, we cannot surpass ourselves. When everything in our life would go well, then perhaps the only decision, in which we could put something of ourselves, would be about the choice of what we will have for dinner that evening. However, essential choices are more likely in a situation with conflict and problems. According to NDEers there are always several possible solutions. There are always different options.

Sometimes we think they aren't there, but then we have to look better and try harder. Sometimes, there really aren't any optimal solutions. An NDEer, for instance, who was a great singer, developed severe health problems and had to stop singing. She told me that she couldn't change anything about this misfortune, but she explained that she still had choices. She could sit down and be very depressed, for which she had every reason. By doing this, she would sap energy from herself and others. However, she chose for another option. She showed people around her that within her setback she could still be radiant and loving to others.

We perform very well when we opt for a solution through which we create positive ripples that add energy to Unity Universe. These are choices that bring greater insight and more growth for all. There-fore, problems, setbacks, and conflicts give us great opportunities to achieve a greater insight and growth for all. All of this is possible in a way that we seem unable to understand right now.

Is this vague? Yes, but we will get a good answer when we meet The Light (but, please, don't commit suicide to get that answer).

Sodom and Gomorrah

At this point I want to deal with a subject that is close to my heart.[33] In B'reshit/Genesis there is a story about Lot, the cousin of Abraham. Since they both travel through an area that is not suited for such large groups of shepherds, they decide to part ways. Lot chooses to enter the region with the cities of Sodom and Gomorrah and to establish himself there with his shepherds. It is mentioned that in that region there is an abundance of water and it is therefore like a garden of YHWH, comparable to the land of Egypt (which was very fertile at that time). Consequently, it is a very wealthy region. While the shepherds pitch their tents in the countryside, Lot goes to Sodom to live in that city. He does that even though "the men of Sodom were exceedingly wicked and sinful before YHWH."[34] They accept Lot in their midst because he is rich.

At the same time Abraham goes in the opposite direction and goes further into the country of Canaan. YHWH informs Abraham that He intends to investigate whether the sins of Sodom and Gomorrah are indeed extraordinarily grave. Should that be the case, He will destroy those wealthy cities. There is then a remarkable dialogue between YHWH and Abraham. Abraham asks if the cities will be eradicated if there are fifty righteous inhabitants. YHWH says that He wouldn't do it if there are this many righteous people. Then Abraham starts to bargain and asks if the city will be spared if there are only forty-five righteous ones. YHWH affirms this. Next, Abraham tries the number of forty and again YHWH affirms that He would spare the cities because of this many righteous ones. Where does it stop? Also, with thirty the cities will be spared, and with twenty and with ten.

Then there is a scene change. Two mysterious envoys of YHWH enter Sodom. Lot, who is at the gate of the city, sees the visitors come and welcomes them. He bows, wants to wash their feet and offers them accommodations so that they can continue their journey the following morning. They refuse, but Lot insists and finally they come along.

After dinner, before they went to sleep, the men of Sodom were jostling each other outside the door. "From young lad to old man, all the people even from the outskirts." Literally the Bible says: "we want to know them!"[35] but that has become to mean that they wanted to have sexual intercourse with the guests.

Lot goes outside and pleads with the people of Sodom to show respect to his guests. Astonishingly, he even offers his daughters for them to have sex with. However, the people of Sodom turn angry. They stir each other up by saying that Lot has come to live in their midst and now acts as their judge. Then they shout at Lot that they will treat him even worse than they intend to treat his guests. This threatening situation comes to an end when Lot's guests strike everyone outside the door with blindness.

After that the mysterious guests urge Lot to leave the city together with his people, since they will destroy the degenerated city. But why should the city be destroyed? What is really the evil of the men of Sodom? It is always told that it is about the homosexual intercourse the men of Sodom wanted to have with Lot's guests. But is that really the reason? Would the whole population of Sodom have been gay? It is implied that everyone, the whole population, seriously fails towards YHWH. How would the population of Sodom reproduce when everyone is gay? Or would that only apply to the men, since there is only mention of men? If that is so, what do the women think of that? And suppose that the women do not seriously fail YHWH (and surely there would be more than ten in the city), would YHWH not keep his promise and spare Sodom? Or would it be that in the opinion of YHWH women do not count? And finally, what about that strange story of Lot wanting to offer his daughters to the men of Sodom? That surely wouldn't work with gay men, would it?

No, there are too many questions about the alleged homosexuality of the city. That cannot be the reason. The real reason is made clear by Ezekiel, one of the great prophets.[36] He explicitly tells us what the sin of Sodom is: "She and her daughters (probably the other cities or villages in the region) were proud, sated with food, complacent in their prosperity, and they gave no help to the poor and the needy. Rather they became haughty and they committed abominable crimes in my presence."

Sodom and Gomorrah were rich cities, because in the pre-industrial, agricultural era wealth was determined by the fertility of the land. And the land was "like a garden of YHWH." The people, however, seriously failed YHWH because they conceitedly took their riches for granted and felt no further obligations. They wanted to keep everything for themselves and didn't want to share anything with others. They were only focused on their self-interest. They accepted Lot only because they didn't have to support him. After all, he was a rich man. Other strangers were not tolerated.

Lot was also a good man, because he was actually good to strangers. He bowed to them, wanted to wash their feet and provided a meal for them. Moreover, he was prepared to offer the chastity of his daughters when the locals came to threaten his guests. In short, he was prepared to share everything with others. The only things the people from Sodom could bring to the fore were their hostility and threats.

Homosexuality is not the reason why Sodom and Gomorrah were destroyed. They were destroyed because they didn't want to share their wealth with others.

SHARE YOUR WEALTH WITH OTHERS

Being rich is not bad in itself. People are allowed to enjoy their wealth. Besides, when YHWH would think that wealth is bad, why did He make Abraham and his cousin Lot so rich? They too enjoyed their wealth. Wealth, however, creates an obligation. We may enjoy it, but we should be prepared to share it with others too. When we take wealth for granted, wallow in it and keep it to ourselves, we are on the wrong track. Then we seriously fail YHWH because YHWH also loves the needy people.

As far as I know it doesn't emerge from NDEs that wealth in itself is bad. Two aspects, however, seem clearly stated by those who have had near-death experiences. The first is that people shouldn't be too attached to wealth. When that happens we may have more difficulty letting go of the world when we die, and we might even get stuck somewhere between heaven and earth. Secondly, we can make people cheerful and happy when we share our wealth with them. In this way we can use wealth to show our love for others. And during our life review we will actually experience the happiness that it can bring. And if we don't share and keep it all to ourselves, we will feel disappointed about having missed an opportunity to bring joy and energy to the world.

Maybe even today we should ask ourselves in the rich West whether we don't resemble Sodom and Gomorrah to some extent. Aren't we to a large extent greedy and focused mainly on our own self-interest, and don't we too lack the desire to share our wealth with the poor and poverty-stricken parts of our world where three billion people live? And within the United States we accept that there are forty million people living below poverty level, equal to the number of people living in the state of California.

On top of that, like Sodom and Gomorrah, some countries such as the Netherlands close their borders to refugees and without a blush send people who have waited for years for a residence permit back to their birthplace. The number of suicides among refugees who are waiting for a residence permit is notably higher than in the rest of the population. We are jointly responsible for that. Couldn't we say that, just like Sodom and Gomorrah, we seriously fail in our duty towards YHWH at this moment?

HOMOSEXUALITY

For many centuries Jews, Christians, and Muslims have all seized upon the chapters on Sodom and Gomorrah to discriminate and belittle homosexuals and to publicly call eternal damnation upon them.[37] They didn't want to see how illogical the story is and they didn't want to see the chapter of Ezekiel at all.

How is homosexuality judged in NDEs? First remember what the most important message that people take back from their NDE is that we should have love for all and everything. Could that also include the love between two men or two women? The answer is YES. There are no restrictions to love.

There have been many homosexual men and women who have had an NDE.[38] While on Earth, some of them have learned to be ashamed of their sexual orientation. To their amazement their homosexuality was not an issue at all during their NDE. It was simply not important. The Light did not seem to be interested in their sex-life, but, instead, is interested in their love-life. And in this case "love-life" should be seen in a very broad sense: how do we fill our life with love for all and everything? Obviously that also includes our partner, regardless of gender.

The Essence of Judaism

Judaism is based on two fundamental principles, namely that there is only one God and that we have to love Him/Her, and that the people is Israel are chosen to bear this belief.[39] It is not explicitly about "spreading" the religion because YHWH didn't ask the Jews to convert others. Nevertheless, eventually it is intended that other people will also convert to that one God.[40] The conversion of heathens will take place because the Jews will be an example to them. That is why Jews have to live a sacred life by living up to the previously described commandments and to the many other "do's and don'ts." One of those do's is that we have to love our fellow man as we love ourselves. This doing well unto others also means doing well to slaves and even animals. They have to be treated well too.

In the Torah there is also little mention of reward or punishment after death. In general there is little about what happens after death. There is belief in a hereafter, because after our death we return to our origin. We go back to the creator.[41] When we have behaved very badly, we will unfortunately be cut off from YHWH.[42] For some time we will have to do penance in the sea of fire, Gehenna.[43] Even though it won't be fun there, it will fortunately not be forever, as the Christians and Muslims believe. There are undetermined periods for a stay in Gahenna. Evil people stay about twelve months (depending on what they did wrong) after which they are still allowed to proceed to the garden of delight (the Gan Eden).[44] This is possible because of YHWH's infinite forgiveness and mercy. This beautiful garden is not only reserved for Israel. Others can also take part in it. Everyone who did well and made choices for the good can go there. with Islam, Mohammed himself has given the initial impetus to spread the religion by sword.

Foolish Fixations

On the issue of spreading Judaism there are no excesses to be mentioned. Judaism does not require the faith to be actively spread. This will prove to be different with both the derived religions, Christianity and Islam, where efforts to convert take a more prominent role. With Christianity it is even a central dogma that people can only go to heaven through Christ, and that is why Christians needed to convert as many people as possible. And with Islam, Mohammed himself has given the initial impetus to spread the religion by sword.

However, for the time being we are busy with Judaism and its foolish fixations. We could be amazed about the many dietary prescriptions and all other do's and don'ts, but it is difficult to demonstrate that this leads to lovelessness and disrespect towards others. However, there is another aspect of Judaism in which more harm is done. That is the fanatic way in which some Jews lay claim to the "promised" land.

It was described how YHWH, on an important crossing of trade routes, reveals Himself to Abram and promises this land to his offspring. It is Canaan, the region just north of Jerusalem. Ever since the establishment of the State of Israel in 1948 this divine promise provides enough of a reason to a large number of Jews to deport the local inhabitants of the land and to appropriate their land and their property. This is an offence against the sixth and eighth and possibly a few other Commandments.

After the start of the Diaspora in AD 70 Jews have always been homesick, a very understandable emotion. At the start of the twentieth century, the homesickness has led to a steady influx of Jews to the land that for millennia had been inhabited by Palestinians. In a written declaration dated November 2, 1917, the British minister of foreign affairs Balfour confirmed to the banker Lord Rothschild that Great-Britain will do its best to facilitate the establishment of a Jewish state. It was added that nothing would be done to violate the rights of the present inhabitants.[45]

The steady increase of Jews in the region accelerated after the Holocaust of the Nazi Regime in Germany. Despite the fine promises in the Balfour Declaration, its aims could not be achieved without consequences for the local people. In 1948 there were 760,000 Jews and 1.4 million Palestinians. Half of the latter have fled or were chased away. This was a kind of ethnical cleansing avant-la-lettre. This is not in accord with the principle of love for your fellow man, ordered by YHWH and confirmed as extremely important by NDEers. However, it would become even worse.

In 1956 during the Suez crisis 275 people were killed by Israeli soldiers in the Gaza strip. "Snipering" and sabotage were used as excuses. Later the Israeli general and war hero Moshe Dayan would say in his memoirs that only once had a Palestinian guerrilla fighter fired out of a house. By saying that, he acknowledged that the violence of the Palestinians was limited and hadn't been on such a massive scale as had been previously presented. Furthermore, he indicated that the plundering by Jewish soldiers and civilians shouldn't be played down. He wrote that it has caused a great deal of damage to the Palestinians and that this was a shame for the Jews.[46]

After the Six-Day War in 1967, Israel occupied the whole area west of the Jordan River. This was the go-ahead for a next phase in the expropriation of the area. Houses of Palestinians were blown up or were bulldozed and Palestinian property was confiscated in favor of the Israelis. The establishment of Jewish settlements on the West Bank were initiated and this was propagated by subsequent Israeli governments with the intention to make it impossible for future governments to withdraw from the land given by YHWH.[47] In particular during the Likud government of Menachim Begin, which started in 1977, the number of settlements exploded. In 1977 the number of settlers was about 55,000 and that had increased to 311,000 by 2010 and the number is constantly growing. In addition, neighborhoods in East Jerusalem were annexed in a move never recognized by the international community. When it is so firmly believed that the land belongs to Israel, why aren't YHWH's commandments obeyed? In several sections of the Bible we are reminded of the terrible life of the Jews in Egypt before Moses led them out of that country.[48] Every year with Jewish Passover that exodus is remembered again. It is then read from the Bible that Israelis shouldn't do as the Egyptians did long ago.[49] They may not treat others in that way. They are called upon not to oppress or mistreat strangers and to treat them as if they were fellow countrymen because YHWH loves strangers (in this case, read: "the Palestinians") just as much as the Jews. Yet it is predominantly the fundamentalist religious groups that support the expropriation and the oppression.

The foolish fixation that the land of Canaan belongs to the Jews has hardened. Sensible arguments to ease the tension and to consider the feelings of the Palestinians have no effect. No one listens, while there are enough good arguments to stop this foolish fixation. What are some of the arguments? I already mentioned the theological arguments: YHWH ordered people to love each other and from that it naturally follows that He/She also ordered people to treat strangers correctly. A more practical argument is that the situation of the Palestinian population is an unbearable and untenable situation. The number of Palestinians is going to exceed the number of Israelis and with that the number of people that will have unrestrained hate against the Israelis will grow. I am afraid that even a wall will then not be enough to guarantee safety.

6

Christianity

LOVE GOD, YOUR NEIGHBOR, & YOURSELF EQUALLY

Three Gods in One

Christians did not adopt the custom of circumcision of men and the dietary laws from the Jewish religion. The only dietary law was the ban on eating meat on Friday, but this ban is rarely observed anymore. It existed out of respect for Jesus who died on a Friday. For the rest virtually all of the Jewish faith was adopted.

Thus the holy scriptures of the Jews form an integral part of Christianity. This is called the "Old Testament." Only the order of some of the books has been reversed in Christian scriptures. One could think that the essence of the Jewish belief was adopted in its entirety too, but that is only partly true. What was adopted were the principles that idols should not be worshipped, that God deserves our respect, that egoism is not considered to be correct, and that we should have respect for our fellow man. This is the shortened version of the Ten Commandments of Moses.

There are differences between the Christian and the Jewish beliefs, of which two are essential. The first crucial difference has to do with the importance attached to the fatal misstep of Adam and Eve: the eating of the forbidden fruit that led to the mortality of men. The second fundamental difference is the recognition by Christians of Jesus as the Messiah, who had already been announced as such in the Old Testament. Through his sufferings He is thought to have erased the original sin of Adam and Eve. His life, his teachings, and especially his dying for humanity are of paramount importance to all Christians.

Chrisos is Greek for "Messiah," which is Hebrew for "The Anointed." Jesus is not only indicated as the long-promised Messiah, but it is very important that He also receives divinity status. As if that is not already stirring enough, the case is made even more exalted: Christianity assumes three divine entities consisting of God the Father, God the Son (Jesus Christ), and God the Holy Spirit.[1] Together this ensemble forms the "Holy Trinity." However, as Christians maintain, these three Gods are not three, but one. They have to say this, in order to meet the requirement of Abraham and Moses that there is but one God. Otherwise Christianity would go down the road towards becoming a pagan religion, like the Roman or Greek religions, where heaven was almost drowning in gods. By stating that those three Gods are actually one, they solved this predicament and were able to maintain that Christianity is, in reality, a monotheistic religion. Three Gods in one is of course something Christians themselves do not understand and cannot explain. That is why they say that it is a "mystery of faith" that cannot be comprehended by common people. Discussion closed.

Nevertheless attempts have been made to simplify this complicated mystery of faith. One of those can be found in the "credo," the Christian confession of faith. It reads: "God from God, Light from Light, true God from true God." This means that if people make something, it will always be something human. But if God creates something, then that will be divine. With that it follows that when God begets Jesus by Mary, logically Jesus has to be divine and not human.

Even so, it remains peculiar because in this way a sort of divine family is introduced, or in fact a dualistic god with a father and a son. Moreover, if you consistently maintain the idea of God creating only divine things, then we are divine too. After all, God made us out of clay and his breath. So what applies to Jesus should also apply to us. And actually, that is what some NDEers say: we all have a spark of divinity in us. We are all part of The Light.

For the Muslims, although not exclusively just them, the Holy Trinity remains highly unfathomable. Mohammed did not accept the divine character of Jesus. He had a much more simple explanation. Mohammed believed Jesus was not a god, but was a normal human being. He was a very important prophet, that is true, but he was definitely not divine. And although he was important, he was of course not as important as Mohammed himself.

Jesus the Son of God

In the beginning Christianity was not a static religion. Its development is a very interesting story with many twists and turns in the defining of who Jesus really was. The first twist occurred in AD 325, where a council in

Nicea (Turkey) was to determine the mutual relationship between God, Christ, and the Holy Spirit. Up to that point, a rather strong religious movement existed that was based on the idea that Jesus is equal to other people, and that He is adopted by God as a son to be the first amongst other human beings. This idea was banned in Nicea where the divinity of Jesus was confirmed. Jesus was promoted to being God. Since then this doctrine is expressed in church services when people pray: "God from God, Light from Light, true God from true God."

In Nicea it was also determined that in God there are three different entities, but that all three are equal and form one whole. Since Nicea, this very complex "whole" is known as the "Holy Trinity." Although it was stipulated that the father (God) and the son (Christ) are equal and of the same substance, it was stated that they are separate persons. If this is not by itself already incomprehensible, then the supplemental dogmas concerning this subject certainly are. The problem remained the person of Jesus, who is both God and man. There was a movement in the East (particularly in Constantinople, present-day Istanbul) in which people believed that Jesus was a kind of dualistic whole, both a human person and a divine person. In this view, Mary was the mother of the human person because a god of course cannot have a human as a mother. In the West, on the other hand, one held onto the opinion that Jesus is not dualistic, but one entity.

In 431 at the First Council of Ephesus (western Turkey) this difference of opinion was solved in a peculiar way. The Western bishops were the first to arrive and locked the doors for the Oriental bishops. Quickly they decided that Jesus was one whole and did not consist of two persons. He was solely God and, therefore, could not also be a human. The consequence was, however, that Mary had to be accepted as the mother of God.[2]

With that coup the matter was not really closed, because the question remained how it is possible that Jesus is God, but even so walked on Earth as a human being and died as a human being. Fortunately, the Council of Chalcedon (near Istanbul) in 451 brought relief: Jesus was indeed one person, but had two natures, a divine one and a human one. However, for certain oriental Christians this so-called "doctrine of the two natures" was too much to bear. Christians in Egypt and Ethiopia (the Copts) have not accepted this dogma and in the Syrian Orthodox Church and the Armenian Church the idea lives on that Mary is not the mother of God.

After another eleven centuries, Protestantism knocked Mary off her divine pedestal too. She was downgraded from being the mother of God to the mother of Jesus. Jesus remained, however, the Son of God. And, after five centuries, Protestantism also renounced celibacy: clergymen could henceforth marry and have children (this was later reintroduced in the Anglican Church as well).

Celibacy, which in the West was established in 1022, is an important doctrine of the Roman Catholic Church. It is often suggested that this was done because Jesus supposedly refrained from sex and that clergymen should follow Jesus in this. But the truth is coarser. Pope Benedict VIII (1012-1024) was afraid that parts of the ecclesiastical possessions would end up through inheritance in the possession of the children and wives of clergymen. In this way an important source of income for the church would disappear.

THE FAMILY OF JESUS

Mary is a virgin; that is a Roman Catholic dogma. She was not only a virgin, but she also remained one after she had borne Jesus. She did not have intercourse at all with her lawful husband Joseph. Despite this dogma, one can read in the gospel of Matthew that Joseph did not have intercourse with Mary until she had borne Jesus. Implicitly, this means that thereafter he might have had a cuddle with her.[3]

Further on in Matthew's gospel this seems to be confirmed, because there it says that not only his mother, but also his brothers wanted to speak to Him.[4] In Mark one can even read that Jesus had three brothers and an unknown number of sisters.[5] He also writes that with two of her children Mary stood watching from a distance how her son was crucified.[6] It is sometimes stated that it is an incorrect translation and that it should refer to the cousins of Jesus, but why couldn't it be the brothers and sisters? Would that make Jesus any less spectacular?

It is strange to see how the Christian Church handles the sexual desires of humans in general and those of Jesus and Mary in particular. Mary is thought to be completely immaculate and to have not had intercourse at all. And the same applies to her son. This idea has developed further over the centuries and it has eventually led to the condemnation of sex. Sex is dirty and it is the consequence of the sin of Adam and Eve, as the important dogmatic theologian Thomas Aquinas (1225–1274) knew with great certainty.

Yet one should wonder whether it is probable that Jesus or Mary didn't have sex. It is true that nothing in the New Testament indicates that Jesus gave in to sex. But neither does anything in the New Testament indicate that He didn't. It has always surprised me that Christians stressed the incarnation of Jesus as something very important, but that they didn't want to accept all the consequences of this. Essential to man are things such as the need for food, the digestion processes that go with it, but also sexual desires that develop during puberty. In the Bible Jesus is actually mentioned as a lover of good food and drink. Consequently, he should have had a metabolism and had to go to the toilet once in a while (which is not mentioned in the Bible either). Then why would He only have had those human properties?

It is interesting that in NDEs sex is never an issue. I don't know of any account of an NDEer who says that sex is bad or that you should only have sex for reproductive purposes, and that you are not allowed to enjoy it. Nor did any NDEer come back who said that sex is a "must," or that we should do it regularly. Sex simply seems to be no issue over there. This has occasionally been stated in so many words.[7] "It seems that The Light and all the other beings of light are not interested in our sex-life. What they are interested in is our love-life, and that is something completely different."[8]

Love is the number one task. It is the love for everyone and everything, and by far most of our love can be given without combining it with sex. It is the love for our family, friends, colleagues, animals—you name it. Of course, some love is closely related to sex. That should be no problem, because it is still love. What about sex when it is not related to love? When it harms no one, it is neutral. Consequently, it can still not be considered a real problem.

However, when sex and love are opposites, we can be sure it becomes a serious problem. Think of rape; think of incest. People who do one of those run the chance of reliving in full detail what the effect on their victim was. And think of having too much of an attachment to sex, so that when one dies and has no body anymore, one might still long for sex. It would then be like any other attachment to the material world that might make it less easy to proceed to the spiritual world.

Original Sin

We have to understand what place "sin" has in the Christian belief system in order to understand who Jesus was and why He has come as a man to Earth to be tortured to death.[9] For that purpose we have to go way back in time, to Adam and Eve. Because what they did was terrible. They ate from the forbidden fruit and by doing that they acquired knowledge of good and evil. With this "original sin" as it is called, they spoiled life and paradise for everybody and wrecked all of mankind.

Adam and Eve had free will. They could have chosen to remain beautiful spiritual creatures, but instead, chose to commit this terrible sin and turn into carnal beings. One of the side effects is that humans have these appalling sexual desires.

Their trespass was so terrible that after birth everyone inherits Adam and Eve's sin. Consequently, everyone earns eternal damnation. It is only correct and understandable that God punishes all future generations and thus all of mankind for that one trespass. God's punishment does not only include that people become mortal, but also that they are damned.

There is only one way to get rid of this original sin and that is by the mercy of God himself. The good news: God is very merciful. The bad news: his mercy is only available for a select group of virtuous people.

If you think that you can try your best to belong to this select group by living virtuously, you are wrong. Only the mercy of God can make someone virtuous. Even when you try to be virtuous, you will not succeed when God doesn't want it. This is miserable, but we shouldn't complain because we should realize that damnation is God's justice after that horrible sin. He has all the right to withhold his mercy and salvation from anyone He chooses. He may choose whom He wants to save.

The ones He chooses have, incidentally, been pre-ordained all along to go to heaven and, therefore, his choice seems to be a bit arbitrary. This part of the doctrine is known as the predestination, which has partly found its way into the background of the Roman Catholic Church, but which is still very much in the foreground of the Protestant and especially the Calvinist beliefs. The truth is that predestination was not introduced by Christ, but was taken from Paul's letters to the Romans in particular.

All these "brilliant" insights about original sin, eternal damnation, as well as the salvation for a select group have been made explicit and were developed by one highly esteemed Christian saint and confirmed by another. The first was Saint Augustine (354–430), who, incidentally, also determined that the world is only six thousand years old. The other was the very influential theologian and philosopher Saint Thomas Aquinas (1225–1274), who was the first scientist who was able to establish dogmatically that witches truly exist. ...

And now the most important part of the doctrine: the salvation of the select group is made possible by Jesus Christ, the Son of God. Through his death He washes away the sins of the select group. That is a relief. The only thing we now need to know is who is in that group.

According to Augustine, heathens are excluded because they were not baptized with water that was blessed by a priest. They will end up in hell where they will burn for eternity in an ever-consuming fire.[10] A similar fate, of course, also applies to children, for whom there was not enough time to perform this most important christening ceremony. It is harsh but fair. Even though they will not have to go to hell proper, they have to stay in an adjacent environment called *limbus*. All of this was derived from what Apostle John revealed. He makes Jesus say: "Verily, verily, I say unto thee, except a man be born of water and of the Spirit, he cannot enter into the kingdom of God."[11]

The Roman Catholics believe that this select group is quite large. When you are baptized and lead a good life in which you don't commit any mortal sins (like abortion or murder), your chances are good. Protestants seem to believe that the group is a bit more limited, although that differs with each Protestant denomination. The reason is that they stress certain passages in the Bible, like "many are called, but few are chosen."[12]

There are some other parts of Augustine's "loving" doctrine worth mentioning. Animals have no immortal soul and will therefore never go to heaven. Sex is only allowed when it gives no pleasure and as long as it is only aimed at the reproduction of man (so that even more damned beings are created). And because reproduction is so important, birth control is inadmissible.

Let's turn briefly back to sin again and compare the Jewish and Christian attitude towards it. Sin also plays a part in the Jewish religion. It is believed that man has a choice to commit sin or to avoid it. When he sins, punishment will follow which can be very severe. The difference is that in Christianity freedom of choice has disappeared. Because of the heritage of Adam and Eve we are born stained with original sin. We can't do anything about that.

JESUS DID NOT MENTION ORIGINAL SIN

The words "original sin" cannot be found in the Old Testament and neither can they be found in the New Testament. Nowhere in the gospels is there an explicit mentioning that it was Jesus's task to wash away the horrific sin of Adam and Eve. The only possible indication occurs when John the Baptist sees Jesus come and says: "Behold the Lamb of God, who takes away the sin of the world."[13]

In the Jewish religion, from which Christianity is derived, the concept of "original sin" doesn't even exist. The concept was developed much later after Jesus's death and welded into a well-conceived doctrine. And why? Because Jesus couldn't have just died for nothing, so they wanted to find a good reason for the suffering and dying of Jesus. Paul, one of the most influential first Christians, who incidentally didn't know Jesus himself, introduced "sin" as a major topic in Christianity. For example, he writes in one of his letters that one man brought sin into the world, and, of course, he meant Adam.[14]

The concept of "sin" is further developed by several Church Fathers and, as mentioned, was more explicitly formulated by Augustine. He even wrote that mankind is a "mass of sin." And without a higher power you cannot get rid of it. Moreover, it is hereditary. And of course, the higher power is Jesus, the savior.

It is possible to think about original sin in terms of reincarnation. Then you would carry sins from a previous life or lives with you. But reincarnation is not something that all NDEers believe in and it doesn't fit into the Christian doctrines. It is sometimes suggested that it originally was part of Christianity because Jesus supposedly alluded to it. One example is when Jesus seems to indicate that John the Baptist is the prophet Elijah.[15] Another example is when Jesus says: "That which is born of the flesh is flesh, and that which is born of the Spirit is spirit. Marvel not that I said unto thee, Ye must be born again."[16] In any case, it is not certain that Jesus tried to introduce reincarnation as a truth. The official view is that He did not.

More important is that in NDEs nothing indicates that people are doomed when they aren't baptized in a Christian way. On the contrary, it is an established fact that The Light is seen by all kinds of people, of all walks of life. It was seen by Christians but also by people of other religions, and also by atheists. Therefore, the mercy of The Light seems somewhat greater than the mercy that God has according to Augustine.

Mercy, however, is probably not the right word either. It is a Christian idea that is connected to the importance they attach to "sin" in general, and "original sin," in particular. NDEers know that something else is far more important than sin and mercy. It is the great love that they feel during their experience and the unconditional and limitless love that The Light radiates. Since we all have a part of The Light within us, we are profoundly interconnected with It. Therefore, we cannot be doomed and we will never be left alone. Even the people who have distressful NDEs and who sometimes even talk about hell-like environments cannot be effectively detached from The Light. From NDEs we learn that the moment we are born we get the right to return again to where we come from, which is the environment where The Light is. It is our birthright. There is no necessity of a baptism or any other religious formality. These are thought up by humans like the two saints Augustine and Aquinas and do not bind The Light in any way.

Something more needs to be said about the distressful NDEs. It is still not clear why some people have these. In some cases these experiences seem to have resulted from a heightened attachment to matter (for instance to money) or from addictions (e.g., alcohol, drugs, sex), while suicides seem not to promote the chance to have a blissful NDE. (Even though many who failed at their suicide attempts have reported distressful experiences, it should be stressed that there are also reports of blissful ones.) Therefore, one could think that distressful experiences are the result of one's own choice. Yet on the one hand, there are cases in which distressful NDEs could not be traced to either of these causes. And on the other hand, there are some cases where NDEers have confessed that they had led a terrible and loveless life (one even with a craving for killing) and yet still had a blissful NDE.

In all cases an NDE will lead to changes in the lives of all those who have had such an experience. For these changes to occur it doesn't matter whether the NDE was blissful or distressful. Any NDE will make people see that living a more loving life and creating positive ripples leads to more fulfillment. In this way a distressful NDE can still be seen as positive. And, I would like to add, I am convinced that everyone will eventually be admitted to the realm of The Light. All roads eventually lead to The Light.

But let's turn back to Adam and Eve. According to the previously mentioned brilliant Christian saints, it was these two people who brought sin into the world. Because of them Jesus was tortured and crucified and died. The interesting question should pop up: How should we see this dogma after Darwin argued that Adam and Eve as actual persons couldn't have existed? Take a moment to think about this.

The Teachings of Jesus

According to the evangelist John, Jesus performed his first miracle at a wedding. The host ran out of wine and Jesus rescued his honor by turning water into wine. Of course, the wine Jesus created tasted much better than the wine the host had served. A wonderful miracle, and after that first one many more would follow. As a "magician" Jesus went around and healed the crippled, the lepers, the blind, the mute, and the insane. At different instances He even raised people from the dead.[17] He also walked on water and twice he multiplied a few loafs of bread and some fish in such a way that a large crowd could be fed.[18]

However, his teachings are more important than his miracles. For a good understanding of this we have to bear in mind that Jesus was a Jew.

This is something that Christians throughout centuries of pogroms and discrimination against Jews have conveniently forgotten. He knew Judaism very well and knew the important laws. He said that He did not come to annul the laws of the prophets. He came to perfect them.[19] Remember that in the Jewish religion there are numerous do's and don'ts, so many in fact that one would almost not be able to see the woods for the trees. When, for instance, He was asked what the most important commandment was in the Law He literally answered:

"You shall love the Lord your God with your entire heart, with your entire soul, and with your entire mind. This is the first and greatest commandment. And the second, equal to it: you shall love your neighbor as yourself. The whole law and the prophets depend on these two commandments."[20]

By answering like that, He combined the most important rule of Jewish religion (love God with all your might) with the essence of the Ten Commandments about the respect for others. He says that living up to these two commandments is better than performing any religious rituals.[21] This is something all NDEers would wholeheartedly agree to. In these two lines He equals the love for God with the love for our neighbors and also for ourselves. Moreover, the love for these three is on an equal footing. What He in fact teaches here is that love is the most important thing there is. If we are looking for the essence of Christianity, then here it is.

From an NDE point of view his other teachings are interesting as well. Don't repay evil with evil, so when someone slaps you on your right cheek, turn the other to him, too.[22] He says that you should love your enemies. And to bless those who curse you. Do good to those who hate you and pray for those who abuse and persecute you. The reason is that it is easy to love your next of kin or friends. Everyone can do that, even bad people can, but it is more difficult to love non-relatives and even enemies.[23] Only then you show perfection in love. This would come close to the perfection of God's love, since God makes no distinction between people. To demonstrate that, it is said that God makes the sun shine on both the bad and the good, and makes it rain on both the just and the unjust.[24] The message is this: perfect love makes no distinction, and thus God loves us all. Now see the resemblance with what is constantly said about The Light in NDEs: its love seems to be total and unconditional, even when we did wrong. It is non-discriminatory; it is there for everyone.

There is another reason why we should give a lot of love to others. Jesus says that there is a relationship between the giving of love and the forgiving of sins. Someone who gives a lot of love shall also be forgiven a lot of sins.[25] When you give a little love, then you will be forgiven for just a few sins. This all happens after regeneration, on "Judgment Day."[26] Christians actually believe that everyone will be judged after their death. However, that will not happen immediately after death, but on Judgment Day when everyone rises from death at the same time and will be judged at the same time.

God himself will not give the Last Judgment, but his Son, Jesus Christ will.[27] He will separate the Good from the Evil. The Good will go to heaven, the Evil to hell. Jesus clearly says that we should not judge others because the measure we take of someone else will also be applied to us. So if we don't want to be judged, we shouldn't judge others.[28] This may be compared with the situation when we are confronted with The Light. During our life-review we will get back what we did to others, and that may also apply to our judgments of others. If we forgive others a lot, we will also be forgiven a lot. "Not until seven times seven you have to forgive your brother, but to seventy times seven," is what Jesus taught.[29] He has stated this even more clearly: "All things whatsoever you would want other people to do to you, you should do that also to them."[30] Or in yet another way: "What you have done for one of the least of my brothers, you have done it onto Me."[31] You could also say that He actually alludes to Unity Universe: I am you, you are me, we are nature.

He also warned us not to become attached to matter. Treasures on Earth are unimportant. They can even prevent you from going to heaven. He once said that it is easier for a camel to go through the eye of a needle, than for a rich man to enter into the kingdom of God.[32] Therefore, share what you have with others.

He taught us to respect others. Other people are important, so serve them, help them, and do something good to them. He says literally: "Whosoever will be great among you, shall be your servant; whosoever will be the highest, shall be servant of all. For even the Son of man came not to be served, but to serve, and to give his life a ransom for many."[33]

PERFECT LOVE

The equality between the love for God, for our neighbor, and for ourselves is a great innovation of Christianity. It is already implicit in the Jewish faith, but the two separate Jewish commandments are integrated into one by Jesus and He elevates the result to become the highest Christian Commandment. Notice that here equality has no bearing on the equality among the three entities, as in Hinduism, but the equality in love we must have for each of them.

Although Jesus stressed the importance of the triangular relation, in His teachings He concentrated on the relation between us all. It is easy to love our partner, our parents, our children or our friends, but that is not enough. We have to love everyone, even our enemies. By doing that, we demonstrate perfection in love. Apparently, the love for all people, without distinction, is the perfect love. According to Jesus that is how God loves, and that is what we should also pursue. He loves all of us because, as a matter of speaking, He lets the sun shine on everyone.

That is how The Light appears in the many accounts of NDEers. The Light makes no distinction whatsoever and loves everyone who comes Its way. Whatever we have done, it is full of forgiveness. That is why even "sinners" may come to The Light.

Some people may think that this cannot be possible for everyone. Being with The Light should only be attainable for those amongst us who didn't "sin" too much, and that people who did "sin" a lot should go to the hell-like environments. Whether that is true, will be very difficult to determine. Among other things it requires a clear definition of "sin" and we need concise ways to measure it. This is impossible.

One can also approach this problem in a different way by starting from the importance of the equality in love between God, others, and ourselves. By giving a lot of love to others and to God, we then draw nearer to them. That won't happen if we barely give love. In the extreme case, if we do not give love at all, we'll be alone. This shouldn't be seen as a punishment but as an essential quality of love. Through love we come closer to each other and to The Light; hate leads to estrangement. In this way we can also see "sin" as a lack of love and "big sin" as the presence of hate. Actually, some NDEers state that sin is an intentional separation from God or The Light.[34] When The Light is considered to be pure unconditional love, sin should then be considered the separation of such love. Indifference is the least harsh form of separation. The harshest form would be hate.

This would mean that when, for whatever reason, we arrive in the hell-like environment, we can escape by radiating love. There seems to be some indications that this is the case. From several accounts it becomes clear that to some extent we can direct ourselves towards The Light. If we wish to find it, we will. It requires, of course, that we let go of our material attachments and that we start longing for love. If we don't do that we might get stuck in a place between heaven and earth.

Here is an example of how someone was able to free himself from the hell-like environment. An NDEer found himself in the "biggest, largest, most vast pit of grayness that one could experience." He was shocked, not only because he felt it was terrible, but also because he instinctively knew that it was real. He decided to calm himself down and with great effort tried to do some meditation. While he was doing this, the color of the place changed. It went to a "rich dark purple." He stresses that the significance of the change of color wasn't merely visual. There was also a change in feeling. He says: "I felt as though a moment ago I'd been faced with someone holding a gun barrel to my head. When the color changed, it was as though he then said, 'Ok, we are not really interested in you,' and took the gun away. I changed from feeling sheer terror, to letting myself think, 'Maybe this won't be so bad.'"[35]

By meditating he made his emotions neutral and he moved from a negative into a neutral environment where there was no hell, but also no Light. There are many more examples in which NDEs started off badly but turned out well. I just want to show that we seem to be able to divert ourselves away from the hellish environment and maybe to direct ourselves into The Light, often just by asking. And if we are there we are safe, because there is not one account in which The Light becomes angry and throws us back into a hellish environment.

From a report of another NDEer it becomes clear that people who are trapped in a hell-like environment are not left to fend for themselves. That applies to deceased people who wander around the earth because they are greatly attached to physical matters (possessions or an addiction, for instance, to sex, drugs, or alcohol), or to those who wander around because they are still thoroughly occupied with their surviving relatives and friends. Or they may be trapped because they continuously undergo the consequences of their suicide over and over again. In all those cases there seems to be beings of light in their immediate vicinity that are ready to lend a helping hand. The only thing that seems to be required is that those people ask for help and accept the help offered.[36]

This seems to have been the case with Howard Storm who has written a book about his fall into hell.[37] While his tormentors were swarming around him he heard a voice (that sounded like his own) saying that he should pray to God. At first he thought it to be a stupid idea, but after he heard the voice a few more times, he tried. He murmured some churchly sounding phrases and even included some lines with reference to God from "The Pledge of Allegiance." This made the demons go mad and they retreated. Since he cited the phrases without real affection, the retreat of the gruesome creatures was all he could realize. However, he felt they remained near. Nevertheless he was alone; he didn't see or feel evil creatures, but there was also no heavenly Light. After he thought for a while about his miserable situation and about his egoistical life that he began to regret, he made a genuine effort to pray. He prayed to Jesus because He was the first person who came into his mind. After all, he was a brought up as a Christian. Then, far off in the darkness, he saw a pinpoint of light rapidly coming closer. When it was near, he saw that it was the one he had been calling for— Jesus—who finally brought him out of his miserable position into The Light.

From these examples we may conclude that when we want to find The Light or the light area, we have to long for it. We have to send our love to it and to ask to be loved. We can be sure that doing that is easier when we have had some experience with loving others during our earthly life, especially when these others are people we didn't personally know. And since we will not have a body when we are dead, we have to show our love solely with our thoughts. The importance of loving thoughts is regularly stressed in NDEs: thoughts are very powerful. If we think about something during our NDE, it will be there. But also on Earth we create with our thoughts. So think of good things, think positively, think of love in general and it will arrive. That is what Jesus also stressed: not only loving actions are of great importance, but also loving thoughts.

The Essence of Christianity

Jesus summarized the essence of the Jewish faith in a few sentences, in which He equates the love for God with the love for our fellow man and for ourselves. This triangle relationship is his innovation and forms the true essence of the Christian faith.

Nevertheless, during his lifetime Jesus particularly stressed one side of the triangle, namely the love for our fellow man. This He repeated many times and in many forms. He said it directly, but also in many comparisons and parables. He also showed it through what He did, for instance by treating prostitutes, foreigners, and tax collectors with respect. In all cases his message in all its repetitions and all its forms kept amounting to the same: love all the people around us!

Apart from that He also stressed that hypocrisy is far from optimal. He often drew a bead on priests and scribes and reprimanded them more than once. He did that especially when they appeared to be stuck in the role of upholding the many religious rules and regulations, and because of this they had lost sight of the most important commandments. For example, He said that doing good had nothing to do with whether or not one eats with unwashed hands, although with Jews that is one of the many commandments. Since He was so harsh against the established religious order, the high priests and the scribes plotted together and urged the Romans to kill Jesus.

That Jesus emphatically stressed loving others and letting good thoughts and deeds arise from our hearts means that people have a choice there. It is of no use to urge people to aim at the good when it is already predetermined that they will do bad things or that they will go to hell. Apparently there is a free will.

Why does Jesus find it so important that man uses his free will to love other people and to think and do good things? He says that if we do that we will enter the "kingdom of heavens."[38] What He actually says is that not everyone can go there. Only those people who fulfill the will of his Father will be able to do so. Apparently the loving of others and the doing and thinking of good things leads to the fulfillment of the will of God.

He is clear about what will happen to the people who do not fulfill the will of God. Sometimes He does that indirectly in his comparisons in which He says, for instance, that the bad branches of a vine will be tossed into the fire. But He speaks about hell in more direct terms too. He says that hell is very hot and that there is wailing and gnashing of teeth. He also says that between hell and heaven there is a great gulf, which makes free traffic from one side to the other impossible.[39]

In short, He says that we have to fear God because He has the power to make us end up in hell. Christians have interpreted this to mean that bad people will first go to Purgatory (in the gulf between hell and heaven) where an attempt will be made to burn off their sins. If it works, they may proceed to heaven. But if the purification process fails, unfortunately they will then go to hell forever.

However, Jesus didn't speak about Purgatory anywhere, although as a Jew He had some idea of hell. Nowhere has He denied or changed the Jewish concept of hell, so we have to take it that He endorsed it. As has been previously discussed, according to Judaism people may be stuck in hell temporarily, but will leave it again after a more or less predetermined lapse of time. Jesus in fact confirms this when He states that the Highest will also be kind to the unthankful and evil.[40] This confirms my conviction that all roads eventually lead to The Light.

Foolish Fixations

Christianity has had many foolish fixations and in my opinion the religion is, unfortunately, still in the middle of many of them. From our present day point of view, it is quite easy to recognize fixations in the past as being ridiculous and there will be some examples of these. Yet it is important to understand that the detection of present-day foolish fixations is very difficult for people who are living right in the middle of them. This observation should also be a warning to us because we may be in the middle of our own private foolish fixations and might not be able to detect how absurd they really are. We should, therefore, always leave room for doubt about our current views and continually ask ourselves whether we are still doing the right thing.

One foolish fixation from the past is the belief that witches exist. These were believed to be evil creatures that regularly went to witches' Sabbaths (feasts with the devil "in the flesh"). They could fly on brooms and do all other kinds of magic (and contrary to what Harry Potter does, the witches in some old Dutch drawings sat on the broom with the brush side in front). The Roman Catholic Church and Protestants officially acknowledged the existence of witches and were convinced that witches were as much an everyday reality as the trees and birds they saw.

Pope Innocent VIII issued a papal decree against witchcraft (in 1484) and ordered witches to be rounded up and destroyed. This led to bursts of intensive raids on people who were thought to be witches. Suspects were horrifically tortured until they could were prepared to admit anything. They then invented the most fantastic and insane stories or agreed to the stories their tormentors wanted to hear. These ranged from their claiming they could change into werewolves, fly on brooms through chimneys, and dance in the shape of a cat with the devil (all actual examples). And they would accuse other people they had met at the witches' Sabbaths, leading to even more arrests. All of this then reinforced the belief in witches and led to an increased "knowledge" about these horrible creatures.

This foolish fixation lasted quite some time, which makes estimating of the number of victims very difficult. There are estimates of hundreds of thousands of victims and the witchcraft scare in Germany in 1629 was supposedly so big that in some areas it is said to have affected 5% of the population. One out of twenty were thought to be witches! The belief in witches was so strong that it took until 1782 before it came to a halt.[41]

Witch scares did not only affect Europeans, but also the Americans. The best example is the witch-hunt in Salem, Massachusetts. A gripping Hollywood movie was made about it. The name Salem was derived from the Jewish word "Shalom" (peace), but during a short period of time there was no shalom in this small town. It started in 1692 when a doctor declared several young girls to be victims of "the evil hand." Scared as these girls were, they accused several other women of bewitching them. These women were subsequently imprisoned, whereupon they accused even more others. Fear and panic started to rule and in one year two hundred people were accused and one hundred-fifty were imprisoned, of which nineteen were eventually hanged.[42]

Another foolish fixation is the firm belief that the earth is the centre of the universe, that there are a maximum of seven heavenly bodies, and that the sun as one of them rotates around the earth. This belief was so strongly defended by the Church that scientists who believed otherwise were intimidated for a long time. They were threatened by the religious police (the Inquisition) with burning at the stake. Galileo avoided this punishment by recalling his theory. Thereafter it still took three and a half centuries for the Church to admit that Galileo was right after all.

Then there are the seven crusades in the 12th and 13th centuries. These were "holy wars" in which the infidels, the Muslims, were to be kicked out of the Holy Land (present day Israel and Palestine). One of the crusader's battle cries was: "God wants it!"[43] Successive popes promised participants absolution and subsequently a full discharge of punishment in the afterlife. This meant that after their death the crusaders would be freed of original sin and any other sin they had committed while on Earth. They would go directly to heaven without having to worry about Purgatory. A wonderful prospect indeed, however, not for those who abandoned a crusade. They would be damned forever. The plenary indulgence was later extended to those who financed the crusades.[44]

Calling for a holy war and giving access to heaven. How could someone have had the nerve to proclaim a war holy or to claim to have the power to give or deny access to heaven? How can a war with its numerous atrocities and its inherent hate between people be the wish of God? And where do they get the right to determine for God who He will allow into heaven? This doesn't come from God, but from their own conviction that they themselves never question or that is never successfully questioned by anyone else. In claiming God's consent for these wars, or for any other war, they ignored God's wish for our total love for all human beings, even our enemies. Worst of all, in claiming God's consent they take up his name for emptiness, violating the third commandment (see previous chapter). However wrong it may be, nowadays we see the calling for a holy war and the giving of access to heaven again in some places in the Islamic world.

Apart from this fallacy, the Crusades were utterly disgraceful for various other reasons, one of these being that even children were used. Another reason is that in God's name the Crusaders not only perpetrated massive cruelties against Muslims and Jews in the Holy Land and also against the Jews in European cities, but also against fellow Christians who lived in present-day Turkey and Syria.[45] The plundering, for instance, of the Orthodox Catholic city of Constantinople (in 1204)[46] was so complete that in her history it ranks the worst event, even worse than the time when the Muslims took the city in 1454 to hold on to her until today. Recently Pope John Paul II asked forgiveness for the Crusades, but since he did this only in general terms, the Orthodox Christians were greatly annoyed. After about eight hundred years they had hoped he would explicitly mention the atrocities of the fourth Crusade.

The teachings of Augustine should also be mentioned. They started a long-lasting foolish fixation. This foolish fixation was the idea that only people who are baptized will have a chance to go to heaven and, for instance, that even babies who die before the christening ceremony will go to a place adjacent to hell. From NDEs we fortunately get a totally different picture. The admittance policy in heaven seems to comprise, in principle, everyone.

Now for some of the contemporary foolish fixations: the first one being celibacy. This was introduced in 1022 for economic reasons, although the official reason for the tightening of the regulations for priests was that Jesus also did not have sexual intercourse. During the Council of Trent (in 1545) celibacy was reconfirmed. This made Protestants go their own way and clergymen were allowed to marry. A second real attempt to change the rigid position was made during the Second Vatican Council (1962-1965). This time, relaxation was generally expected. However, when the subject was just about to be discussed, Pope John XXIII died. His successor, Paul VI, allowed the council to make decisions on many different topics, but not about celibacy. He wished to decide on that alone and with his papal authority he decided to continue the situation. The consequence of his "coup" was that nowadays almost no young people desire a religious career within the Roman Catholic Church and that a few old priests and bishops conservatively manage this institution.

The worst current foolish fixations, however, are the conservative standpoints on morality. The one that has led to the biggest suffering and hardship is the ban on contraceptives. They are considered unethical and Catholics are not allowed to use them. This rigid standpoint is, in part, the cause for the overpopulation in many developing countries where Catholicism had the greatest influence on people. The consequence is an unsustainable strain on nature and a disgraceful poverty in a large part of the world. The reason given for the ban is the respect for life required by God, and his demand to multiply which He issued after the Flood (also think of Augustine's assertion that sex is only allowed when it is aimed at the reproduction of man).

One should think that we have successfully lived up to God's demand to multipy since the population in the world has increased to over 7 billion people. However, we were not successful in our respect for life. In the world there are 46 million people infected with HIV, most of them in Africa, where they have virtually no access to the required medicine. The virus is especially contagious for the sexually active part of the population. The consequence is that the economically important part of the population is endangered. There are places where this part of the population has been largely wiped out and where children and grandparents have to take care of each other.

The epidemic could have been curtailed if condoms had been allowed because these could have curtailed new infections. Instead of lifting the ban, it was reinforced. Pope John Paul II did this on more than one occasion. In addition, the head of Family Affairs of the Vatican has said that a condom does not protect against HIV, which, of course, is a lie.[47]

Maybe this foolish fixation will end some day and some pope in the future will then make apologies for this grave mistake. The question is how long that will take. With Galileo it was three and a half centuries.

∽ 7 ∽

Islam

VOLUNTARY SUBMISSION LEADS TO PEACE & SECURITY WITH ALLAH

The Primeval Book[1]

"There is no other God than that One, and Muhammad is his prophet." Say this confession of faith three times out loud in the presence of others and we become a Muslim. By the way, it has to be in Arabic. This conversion seems to be much easier than in Christianity, where we first have to be baptized (otherwise we end up in hell). Yet the exclamation of this sentence is in itself not sufficient. We must really submit ourselves to Allah. Only then do we become Muslim. Islam, therefore, means something like "entering into a condition of peace and security with Allah through voluntary and complete submission." Although in this sense the word "Islam" seems to be very important, it occurs only eight times in the Koran. The cognate word Muslim ("the one who submits") occurs somewhat more often: forty-four times. However, the word belief or believer is really very popular. It occurs about seven hundred times in the Koran.[2]

Islam is about the total, sincere, and voluntary submission to Allah—the Most Merciful and Most Compassionate—through which we achieve peace within ourselves and with Allah. The question is to whom do we dedicate ourselves? There are no pictures of Him because it is completely forbidden to make them. Allah cannot be comprehended by human beings and cannot, therefore, be depicted. With the limitations of our world, we will never be able to understand the complete character of Allah. Therefore, every impression we have of Him falls short.

In order to gain some understanding of the One to whom we should completely submit ourselves to, Islam allows us to describe Allah in words. We may give Him the most beautiful names.[3] And there are quite a few. The Ruler of Judgment Day. The most powerful. The One Who hears. The One

111

Who sees. The One Who knows. The Wise. The Magnificent. The Hallowed. The Best of the supporters. The One Who accepts remorse. The Respectable. The Lord of dawn, the King of men. The Lord of the throne. The One Who watches over you. He loves people who do well. He is the Salvation. The Giver of security. The Watchful. The Creator. The Maker. The Designer. The Elevated. The Immense. The Allied Who makes the dead live and Who is mighty over everything.[4] And so on, and so on … There are ninety-nine of these beautiful names for God (therefore, in the Islamic rosary, the Subhah, there are ninety-nine beads). Normally, however, He is referred to by the term Allah, which is a contraction of Al-illah, the One Deity.

The numerous beautiful names show that words cannot describe Allah. This reminds us of Hinduism, where Brahman also has a lot of names, but also of what NDEers say. When asked, they too do not succeed in describing The Light. It is simply inexpressible.

Muhammad states that the Jewish religion and Christianity have the same origin as Islam. All three come from Allah's primeval book, also referred to as the mother of the three books.[5] According to Muhammad the Torah and the Gospel are revelations of Allah and in both of them there is "guidance and light,"[6] but what the Jews and Christians made out of it, is not in accordance with the original anymore.

The Jews don't acknowledge both Muhammad and Christ as great prophets, and that is one of the reasons why they are considered to be on the wrong track. In Christianity, Christ is promoted to be one and equal with God and that in the view of Muslims disqualifies Christianity as a monotheistic religion. For their part, The Jews and Christians say that Islam goes astray. The recognition of Christ as prophet makes Islam unacceptable to the Jews, and *not* recognizing Christ as God makes Islam unacceptable to Christians. In this way, everyone is unacceptable to each other. This is a perfect situation for a lot of problems.

Although Jews and Christians see this differently, Muhammad is convinced that he brings us the purified form of the Jewish and Christian religions. According to him, both Moses and Jesus have tried to do that as well, and they are great prophets even though they have succeeded only partially. Of course, Muhammad is the greatest prophet since he succeeds in perfectly conveying the real belief. That is to say, Islam is the perfection of the primeval religion that Allah wanted. Outside of this, nothing can be accepted.[7] And to make sure that after him no one can claim that status, Muhammad declares that he is the last prophet.

ALLAH, MOST MERCIFUL, MOST COMPASSIONATE

According to Muhammad the most beautiful names belong to Allah. He is, among other names, the Most Merciful, Most Compassionate and that is repeated at the beginning of every Sura. His other name is ar-Rahman, the Merciful.[8] Islam regards mercifulness as one of the greatest ideals and it is often combined with justice. People are encouraged to try to be like Allah: just and merciful.

Apart from that, He is full of forgiveness, as we shall shortly see. When a man did something wrong, and he puts something good in the place of it, Allah will be full of forgiveness.

NDEers are convinced that The Light is full of mercy and in none of the NDEs is it mentioned that The Light was angry. On the contrary. It is always full of compassion and understanding. What is also remarkable is that there never is any punishment. It is also often said that the life review is not meant to be a punishment. That it has the effect of a punishment is due to the NDEer himself. He or she feels imperfect in comparison with The Light that emits so much mercy and forgiveness. This usually makes the NDEer feel ashamed of what he has done to others.

The Light remains full of compassion for people who feel ashamed during their life review for what they did to others. It even has compassion with people who are in the hell-like environment. One who reported on what he saw in hell-like environments said that beings of light are continuously present and can offer help to souls who want to leave their deplorable situation. It seems as if they only have to ask and then the beings of light can swing into action.[9] In this sense The Light fully matches the description of Allah as the Most Merciful, Most Compassionate.

Important in the Koran is the encouragement of people to try to imitate Allah. Knowing that this encouragement is in the Koran, it is remarkable that some Muslims do not even want to try to be as compassionate and merciful as Allah, considering the immense hatred they bear for dissidents. However, to justify their terror, they can refer to other texts from the Koran.

From Adam and Eve to Ibrahim (Abraham)

Muhammad partially follows the Torah. Allah made Adam and Eve from earth. It is explicitly stated that all other people after them are made from earth too and that they will return to earth again.[10] From this it can be concluded that we turn into matter when we are born and withdraw from it after our death. This is consistent with the interpretation of death by NDEers: we put on a material coat when we arrive on Earth, and we take it off again when we die. It is interesting that the Koran also says that after our death we will once again rise from the earth. This is a once-only reincarnation on Judgment Day. Christians also believed (and some still do) that there is a physical resurrection on Judgment Day.

Noah, Lot, Abraham, and Moses appear in the Koran, too. Just as in the Jewish Bible, the flood in the story of Noah is said to be Allah's punishment of the unbelievers. With Lot's story immoral behavior is condemned, especially the sexual lust with which men look at each other.[11] This normally is regarded as a condemnation of homosexuality (see the comments in the chapter on Judaism).

Ibrahim (Abraham) is considered in Islam as the most important person. That is to say, he is the most important after Muhammad. Muslims not only consider Ibrahim to be the most important person of ancient times, but so do Jews and, therefore, Christians. The three religions regard him as the common great-great-great-grandfather, the common patriarch. Ibrahim is the first one who adheres to monotheism. Since Ibrahim has a deep-rooted belief in one almighty God, according to the followers of Islam, he is the first man to have completely submitted himself to Allah. Therefore he is the first "Muslim," the first "submitter."[12] Note that Ibrahim apparently became Muslim without having exclaimed three times in the presence of others the first sentence of this chapter, the sentence in which Muhammad takes such a prominent place.

Musa (Moses)

For Muslims, Ibrahim is the first and greatest God-seeker, but Moses (Musa) and Jesus (Isa) are also recognized as great prophets. They, however, are just great prophets, and neither one of them is more important than Muhammad who is all alone at the top.

The story of Musa largely follows the story from the Jewish Bible, but with a lot less detail. For example, Muhammad says that Musa receives the tablets of the Law, on which no one less than Allah himself has written admonitions and clear explanations. However, it is amazing that Muhammad doesn't say exactly what was written on those tablets and what precisely those admonitions are. Neither does he mention anything about the bombastic way in which Musa received the Ten Commandments. There is nothing about the smoke, the clouds, the fire, the thunder, the lightning, the sound of trumpets, and the earthquake. Nevertheless, in the Koran there are rules for the believers, which are somewhat similar to the Ten Commandments.

RULES FOR BELIEVERS

In the Koran there are specific rules for believers, but they only partly coincide with the Ten Commandments of Moses.[13] There is no clear numbering in the Koran, but like in the Ten Commandments the first few rules that are mentioned are, of course, about Allah. We are not allowed to have other gods beside Allah and we have to worship only Allah. The next rules are about our parents. We have to look after them when they are old and we have to address them with respect.

Although it is stated that Allah will supply generous support to whom He wants, there are rules that dictate that we have to give to relatives, the needy, and travelers what they need. Apparently we have a function as an intermediary of Allah. We are summoned not to be stingy, but at the same time there are some interesting escape clauses. One is that we have to achieve the right balance, since if we give too much away we won't have anything left for ourselves. Moreover, we'll then become a squanderer and thus ungrateful to Allah. We have to realize that gratefulness for what we have is, in a way, equal to being a believer (more about that later on). Also, in an admonition it is said that if we can't give something, or when we don't want to, we at least have to say some friendly words to the needy person.

Then there are rules banning the killing of people. The first rule that prohibits killing has to do with killing our own children. Apparently that happened too often in Mohammad's days. When we cannot feed them, we are still not allowed to kill them. "Killing them is a major offence." This sounds good. Another rule states that we may not kill other people because Allah has declared life inviolable. Sounds good too. Nevertheless, there are some cases in which we are authorized to kill. But when you kill while not being authorized, the victim's relatives are allowed to take revenge. It is not explicitly mentioned in the Koran that this revenge can take place by killing the perpetrator, but in any case it is interpreted in this way. Therefore, to some degree killing seems to be acceptable in Islam, but this is contrary to what NDEers say. They have the very strong feeling that killing someone, including oneself, is not at all in alignment with The Light.

Disbelievers

Belief is one of the themes that Muslims attach great emotional value to. The Koran mentions the words "belief" or "believer" about seven hundred times. But what is belief? Is that the belief in Allah? Or is it the belief in Allah and his prophet, or the belief in Allah, his prophet and what the prophet has said on behalf of Allah? For Muslims the latter applies, but one can seriously doubt whether the Koran really means that.

The message of the Koran is made explicit in Sura 17 (verses 9–11). There it says that the Koran leads to the right way, that a big reward awaits for "believers who do salutary deeds" and that Allah has prepared a "grievous penalty" for those who do not believe.[14] The "believer who does salutary deeds" is mentioned more often in the Koran. Therefore, this has to be important.

BEING UNGRATEFUL IS BEING A DISBELIEVER

Let's first establish that people who do not believe in Allah or his prophet are still able to meet The Light after their death. It was not apparent from any NDE that The Light would be disgruntled should the individual not believe in Allah or his prophet, or in YHWH, God or Jesus. In principle everyone, also atheists, are welcomed into The Light. Therefore, believing is not a precondition.

Believing, however, is a very important word in Islam and also in Christianity. In Islam this word is typically used to express the belief in Allah, his prophet, and what his prophet said. Disbelieving is bad, which makes a disbeliever evil and someone we can easily look down upon. But another interpretation is possible and it is one that makes much more sense.

We have to take a look at the longest Sura, number 2 (verse 34). There it is said that after Allah created Adam, He required his angels to prostrate before this new creature. All angels do that, except Iblis. He refuses haughtily and becomes one of the "kafirin." This is the word that is always used to refer to "disbelievers." And Iblis became the greatest of the disbelievers, because he turned into the devil. But it is odd that Iblis, while being so near to Allah, suddenly doesn't believe in Allah. Apparently, someone who knows that the One Allah exists can still be a "kafirin."

In addition, the disbelief of Iblis has nothing to do with Muhammad because Mohammed was not around when Adam and Eve were created. Therefore, belief or disbelief is independent of the Islamic religion.[15] That also seems to be the case in Sura 2 in verse 112, where it says that there will be a reward from Allah for whomever "submits his whole self to Allah, and is a doer of good." This can apply to everyone and also to someone who adheres to another religion in which Allah coincidentally has another name.

Therefore, there has to be a different meaning to the word "disbeliever." And there is, because "kafirin" in principle means "ungrateful." So then what is said in the Koran would become something like: "When you are ungrateful to Allah, there will be a punishment. Only when you are grateful and do salutary deeds, will you receive a reward."

This interpretation is in line with how "kafirin" is used elsewhere in the Koran, for instance when Musa kills an Egyptian. The pharaoh calls him "ungrateful" and uses the same word "kafirin."[16]

Can we do something with this when we consider NDEs? In chapter 2 about NDEs it was argued that life is a very valuable gift and for that reason we should never kill someone, not even ourselves. When we do that we are ungrateful for the gift that Allah gave to us.

It is perhaps easy to see our own life as a gift to ourselves. But what about the life of someone else? Is your life a gift to me? Is my life a gift to you? Absolutely yes, because that is the whole idea we can derive from NDEs. Everyone around us is valuable. There are no lesser souls. Everyone has a function and a place. Everyone has an important task or mission. The importance cannot be measured with an earthly scale. Even what we might consider as unimportant people, are immeasurably important to The Light.

When I kill you, I am ungrateful to The Light and to you for your presence and your contribution to all sorts of things on Earth. Also the lives of people, who cause us a lot of problems and who we might even hate, are still valuable. The fact is that the problems caused by other people give us the possibility to react. There are many alternative reactions possible and it is important to choose the reactions that create positive ripples. These are the reactions that give others and us the greatest increase of energy and thus the biggest positive development. In our reaction we can show our compassion and the greater our compassion is, the better it is for us and for Unity Universe. In that sense Musa would have done better to let the Egyptian live.

Ungratefulness has to do with a lot more than the killing of others or ourselves. From NDEs we can understand that we should be very grateful for our life and for everything that goes with it, both the positive and the negative things, because they create opportunities to expand our compassion. But being grateful is easier said than done, especially when we are in the midst of big problems. And what happens when we are ungrateful because we are disappointed and angry about these big difficulties in our life? What will be the reaction of The Light? Will The Light have prepared a "grievous penalty"?

Absolutely not. There are no reports that The Light told anyone that he or she had been ungrateful, or that The Light became angry or disgruntled when people think of themselves as ungrateful. On the contrary, it seems that The Light never gets angry at all; it is full of forgiveness and acceptance. Also the hell-like environment seems not to be meant as a punishment. It seems that even beings of light have deep compassion for people who are in a hell-like environment, or who are trapped in a state of limbo and for that reason wander around between heaven and earth. In these cases beings of light are ready to help, but seem not to be able to help unless explicitly asked to do so.[17]

Love of Allah

While in the Jewish Bible and in the Christian Gospel the love of God for humans takes a central position, it is as if this is not the case in the Koran.[18] Superficially this seems true, but when we take a closer look, the love of Allah becomes very clear after all.

Every Sura starts by referring to Allah as "Most Merciful, Most Compassionate." That Allah is very merciful is one of the main themes in the Koran. It is even written that He has "inscribed for himself the rule of Mercy."[19] For that reason it is no surprise that Allah's other name is ar-Rahman, the Merciful. Moreover, He is often called "the Forgiving" because Allah says: "If anyone has done wrong and has thereafter substituted good to take place of evil: Truly, I am Oft-Forgiving, Most Merciful."[20]

Allah is not only forgiving. He is also full of compassion and mildness, restrained in anger, and a lot more of these wonderful things. Moreover, it is said that He is all of this in the highest degree. To Him belong the most beautiful names with which we started this chapter. Someone who has so much mercy for people, and who is full of forgiveness and compassion, has to love people infinitely.

And yet, the Koran makes a distinction. Allah loves people who are believers, do good, are patient, and who fight for his cause.[21] I'm afraid that many have already used this often as an argument to justify violence against dissenters and that it will be used often for that purpose in the future.

Allah doesn't love the disbelievers, the ungrateful, the sinners, the haughty, the proud, and the people who are only occupied with earthly matters. Moreover, He is stern, because He is "strict in punishment" and for disbelievers He has prepared a painful punishment.[22]

The Last Day and Then Heaven or Hell

Another important part of Islam is the belief in the final judgment at the end of times. That will be on the Day of Resurrection or also the Day of Judgment. When that day dawns, Allah will come to judge everyone. The procedure is as follows. First everyone will be raised from the dead.[23] That may sound strange, but that is how it is. By the way, Christians officially also still believe in the physical resurrection of the dead body. Then every human is brought before Allah and everyone gets an individual process. Everyone will have to account for his or her own deeds. No one can say something in favor of someone else: the friend cannot say anything for his friend, the father not for his son and a child not for his father (nothing is said about women, but be sure that they will be judged too). We have to stand up to it all by ourselves, alone. Also our possessions on Earth, even if they are numerous, will not help us.[24]

Everything we have ever done is evaluated because "to every soul will be paid in full of its deeds."[25] The punishment for disbelievers is in proportion to the evil they caused, but the ones who did salutary deeds while being a believer don't have anything to fear. For those the reward will be many times greater than the salutary effect of what they did. Allah administers justice very accurately. For that there will be pairs of scales that will be accurately calibrated. Every bit of good and every bit of evil will be paid back. We could wonder how Allah knows everything for certain, but there is an easy answer to this. He is helped in an interesting way because our own ears and our own eyes will be witness to what they have heard and seen.[26] It goes even so far as saying that our own skin will testify to what we have done.[27] This means that we actually know ourselves what was and what wasn't beneficial. In that sense we judge ourselves! Realize that here we have a clear similarity with NDEs. It is even said literally in the Koran: the evil people (the disbelievers) will be witnesses against themselves.[28]

More can be said about the accuracy with which Allah goes about this measurement process. It is not only the case that every little bit of good or wrong will be repaid, but it will be done in such a way that we will feel ourselves how good or how bad it was: "Then shall anyone who has done an atom's weight of good, experience it. And anyone who has done an atom's weight of evil, will experience it."[29] This is astonishing, because this is exactly what NDEers say. The effect of all you have done for or against others you will feel in full yourself. All the sorrow and all the pain, and all the happiness and all the love—everything is shown to us in all intensity, in all detail, and in all nuances. And we shall feel this as if it happens to us.

Apart from the fact that we feel what we have done to others, the judgment will be one of two possible outcomes: a good or a bad one. The good outcome is that we may proceed to the Garden of Paradise; the bad one is that we go to Dshahannam, or hell.

Let's start with heaven or Paradise. There are seven heavens, ordered in layers.[30] Fortunately women can also go there under the same preconditions as men, but only when they are believers and have done salutary deeds.[31] Equality at last!

In Paradise everyone will be maintained and no one will be presented a bill. Quite a reassurance, and moreover we may stay there forever. It is also a nice place to stay for another reason. Paradise has everything that people who know the harsh sides of the Arabian Desert would long for. There is plenty of water that flows in abundance and is sprinkled. There is no insufferable heat or cold. In particular, there is lots of lush vegetation with gardens and oases in which trees offer a plenitude of shade. Bunches of fruit hang low, so we can pick and eat them without straining ourselves. There are not only rivers of imperishable water, but also rivers of milk that stay fresh, and rivers of wine and of purified honey. There also are wines, but the wine that is poured doesn't make our head heavy and does not make us flush. There is silverware and there are crystal glasses with which we can drink from the source, Salsabil. We are dressed in green silk and brocade and wear silver or golden bracelets with pearls.[32] The non-material rewards in Paradise are also worthwhile. For example, there is security and there is no tiredness. Neither will we be exhausted as we are on Earth. Sorrow is taken from us, and in addition resentment is also taken from us.[33]

There are a lot of different compartments in Paradise. There is a part where there are ordinary couches to sit on, but in another part there are richly embroidered settees. Only people who have done very well on Earth are allowed there. Of course, they will be nearest to Allah. They lay there opposite each other and have only serious topics of conversation: the whole time they will say "hail, hail." Young attendants of perpetual freshness will serve them. These attendants are described in a titillating way as scattered pearls. They come with bowls and cans filled with a clear white drink from a special source, which means they don't get hangovers. The inhabitants of Paradise get the meat of birds and can eat from it as much as they want.[34] The young attendants of perpetual freshness are not the only ones to serve us. There are also companions pure and holy with big and lustrous eyes who are just like well-guarded pearls.

And now on the left side there is Dshahannam.[35] Between hell and Paradise there is a separation. Hell also has seven gates with guards.[36] All of this is necessary to prevent villains who are in hell to just slip unseen into heaven. But it also prevents the people in Paradise from going through this barrier to help someone who is in hell. This resembles the description of some NDEers: the beings of light cannot unilaterally rescue souls out of the hell-like environment.

It's no fun in hell. The people there are tied with heavy chains with a length of seventy yards and they are flogged with a whip of iron. There is growling, moaning, and rattling. It is terribly hot because hell consists of impenetrable fire. There is an extensive glowing of flames where people roast in a hell heat. They wear clothes made of fire and as if that isn't enough, a boiling hellish fluid is poured over them. You'd think everything would be over quickly, but when the skin has been baked, they just receive a new skin and so the torture can continue.[37]

People who are in hell are kept alive because they get something to drink and to eat. The drinks are not cooling, but are a soup of a boiling hellish and smelling fluid. The water is like molten metal, which roasts the faces. That water also has the property to cut the intestines. And what they get for food is not much better: it chokes them. It comes from the tree Zaqqum, with sheaths that look like devil's heads.[38]

Once we are there we cannot escape. Each time we want to flee for terror we are brought back to these tortures.[39] And it lasts a long time—for eternity. This is in accordance with the Christian faith, but it deviates from Judaism, in which the torture lasts only a certain period of time.

OUR OWN SKIN

In the Koran it says that our own eyes, ears, and skin will testify about what we have done on Earth. So just like in an NDE we will judge ourselves, and everything we did will be exposed because our senses were there! And on top of that, what we did to others we will feel as if we did it to ourselves. That is the most direct way to become conscious of what we did: to experience ourselves what the effects of our acts were.

There is something more about the peculiar regeneration of our skin in hell. When we arrive in hell, our skin will burn time after time. Each time it is consumed by the fire we get a new one that is subsequently burned again. It is also stated in the Koran that we cannot escape from this regeneration because we are brought back over and over again to the same torture. That is also what is reported by some

NDEers: the unfortunate souls seem to be stuck in an unfortunate trap where the torture resembles a mental torture. For example, some people who made suicide attempts would run around in a small circle to relive their unsolved problem time after time.

Although the beings of light cannot unilaterally rescue souls out of the hell-like environment, the situation doesn't seem to be totally hopeless. A rescue seems possible when both sides desired it. Some NDEers say that help is always nearby. It is supposed to come from the many beings of light who wait until they can swing into action. They are ready, which would mean that the final decision for an actual rescue is up to the unfortunate souls.[40] It seems to be their initiative. But what can they do to show their initiative?

To some extent we may compare this kind of rescue with rescuing someone who is drowning in the water. We can offer a helping hand, but we can only pull him out of the water when he too stretches out his hand. Since after death we have no arms or hands, both sides have to rely on their spiritual strength. This strength depends only on their power of love. In a way the outstretched hand can be compared with the love that flows from the beings of light. That would mean that the victim should grab that love. This means that they need to direct themselves towards love. And this is what becomes clear from many NDEs where the distressful part of the experience changes into a nicer experience. We seem to have a choice: if we have a wish for light and a wish for love, it will be there. Show your love, think of love, and the distressful and fearful feelings will disappear.

Not only was Mohammad's description of hell partly right, his description of heaven is quite good too. Some NDEers also see splendid landscapes with trees, plants, flowers, waterfalls, grass, birds, butterflies, horses, houses and buildings, and everything with absolute stunning colors. Hopefully he was not correct all the way. The part where we will be lying in couches saying "hail, hail" doesn't seem particularly appealing. And, according to NDEers, with respect to the temperature of hell he was quite wrong. In general, the hell-like environment is described as a cold and loveless environment rather than a hot place with a lot of fire where there is something like liquid metal to drink.

Predestination

One of the special characteristics of religions is that they are very capable of finding explanations for dogmas that contradict each other. Christians believe in one God, but also had to make sure that there was a place for Jesus as Son of God without compromising monotheism. And therefore in 325 they resorted to the dogma of the "Holy Trinity." Muslims have their own contradictory dogmas too. These have to do with predestination and the consequences for each individual.

Predestination is that your fate is already fixed and that you cannot do anything about it; things develop as they are predetermined. In the Koran it says that Allah has tied every man's fate to his neck and that He has predetermined everything. It is also written that there is no disaster on Earth or in a man's life without it having already been written down by Allah before the earth was created. As well as determining who will get adversities, He also determines who will have good fortune. He determines whether a woman will give birth to a boy or a girl and He determines for all of us the moment that we will die. We cannot advance this, nor can we extend it.[41]

In itself predestination is not the problem. We cannot prove it scientifically anyway. The problem is that God fixes everything. Apparently He determines in advance that people do evil things and even which evil things they will do. Worse still, this apparently is according to his wish. Without his wish these evil things would not occur because according to the Koran, Allah has a hand in everything. He is continuously managing his creation. From the first day: "Your Lord is Allah who created the heavens and the earth in six days and after that established himself on the throne, from where He governs the world." It is understandable that Muslims exclaim all the time "Insh'Allah," meaning "if Allah wants it." Because without his explicit wish you are not going to the market, you don't drive to work, you don't occupy yourself with religions, and you don't read this book.

This shows the problem with predestination. Firstly, it is Allah who predetermines our fate and apparently wishes some of us to do evil things. Secondly, He is going to give these people an eternal punishment for the evil deeds He wanted them to do. Something similar can be seen in the following example. It was Allah's wish that Jews and Christians would go astray.[42] There could have been only one religion if He had wanted it, but apparently that was not his wish. Therefore, it seems to be his wish that the Jews and Christian go astray and consequently will not go to Paradise.

Fortunately Muslims found a solution. It is still difficult to understand what that precisely is. Muslims themselves also find it difficult to reconcile both extremes, and informally the debate is still ongoing. The formal answer to this dilemma has to do with the existence of two levels of acting.[43] The first level is that Allah puts many possibilities in each individual. The second level is that each man acquires from these possibilities and makes them his own. For this choice he is accountable. It is this freedom of choice that Allah will address on the Day of Judgment. But if this is so, then it still seems that Allah does not have a hand in everything and that our fate is therefore not fixed at all.

One can question whether Muhammad himself wanted to launch the extreme idea of predestination. Maybe he just wanted to indicate that Allah is extremely powerful and capable of fixing someone's fate. The statements are made by Muhammad and cannot be neglected, but we have to realize that the doctrine of predestination got its present absolute form nearly three centuries after Muhammad's death. To complete the comparison with Christianity: the Holy Trinity also came into existence three centuries after Jesus's death. Jesus didn't mention such a trinity at all.

A FIXED TASK AND A FREE WILL

In NDEs there is also something of this dilemma too. On the one hand NDEers say that we have a task or a mission that we all seem to receive before we are born. This task has been agreed upon with us in advance because some seem to remember their task when they are in the middle of their NDE. How that is exactly, is not completely clear, but it is certain that there are fixed tasks in our life that we have to fulfill. The impression we get out of NDEs is that we will be able to fulfill these tasks under normal circumstances because we are invisibly led to do so. Something like that looks a bit like predestination.

However, generally NDEers are also convinced that we have a free will because we always have options we can choose from. We can choose between loving and loveless actions. In addition, our choices are always very important to Unity Universe because they create ripples that travel through this universe. They do something; they have an effect somewhere. For instance, when we all want war, our negative ripples will materialize into something aggressive. When enough people are focused on their short-term self-interest, it will materialize in a financial destruction, something like what we have experienced in the last few years.

The fact that we can create these ripples makes clear that we have a creative power within us. We should be conscious of our creative power and use it in the best way possible. This is because if we would all create positive ripples through our loving actions and thoughts we could even create heaven on earth. It really is possible.

However, sometimes it seems as if we have no choices at all. An example is when we are extremely ill or when some other misfortune strikes us. We don't have a choice there. But also in these situations do we have options we can choose from. We can choose to be depressed and therefore send depressing ripples through universe. But we can also choose to have another kind of emotion. Despite our misfortune we can still try to radiate love and consequently be a joy for the people around us. In this way we are able to create strong, positive ripples.

In this light we might also see the dilemma in Islam. Allah creates the possibilities or options that we can choose from. This means that when no options are created, we have no choice. But when options are created, it would be best for us (and universe) to go for the positive ones. These are the loving actions and thoughts, which are the so-called "salutary deeds." We have more options than we often think, and especially in times of problems there are many options. This means that particularly in those times we can practice our love and compassion by doing "salutary deeds."

The Essence of Islam

It is amazing how well the essence of Islam agrees with the essence of Christianity and Judaism. In Islam there are several central themes. The first theme is the unity of God: there is only one. That theme is repeated in many places in the Koran. It is hammered into the heads of the readers. He is unique. He is all-embracing and He is almighty. A human will never be able to understand how great Allah is and therefore it is strictly forbidden to depict Him. Any depiction would fall short of his Being. We may describe Him with words, and for that we should use the most beautiful words. The most important word is "Merciful" with which each Sura starts to indicate Him (except Sura 9).

With the idea of one God, Islam follows Judaism; or rather, Islam follows Ibrahim, the patriarch from whom the Jewish people descend as well as the Arabs. According to Islam Christians follow a God who consists of three entities. Muhammad believes that Christians are completely off target. Or, as it is implicitly stated in the first and most quoted Sura: they are astray.

The second theme is divisible into two parts. Just like Ibrahim, man has to be a "God-seeker" in the first place. In the second place he must do good deeds. To be a God-seeker, we have to submit unconditionally to Allah. We have to accept everything that He wants to happen to us. We have to trust Him completely and be fully dedicated to Him. In short, we have to believe in Him. Whoever doesn't completely submit to Him, doesn't completely believe in Him. Also the word "ungrateful" has been brought in connection with "unbelieving." Apparently we are ungrateful when we don't completely submit to Him.

By submitting completely to Him, we get our own specific relationship with Him. There is of course already a relationship between Him and us because He knows what is in the hearts of the people. In the Koran it says that He is closer to us than the carotid artery.[44] But that is a unidirectional relationship. By submitting to Him the relationship becomes reciprocal and we start to feel his presence. An individual reciprocal relationship with Allah is the highest objective of submission. By believing in Him like this, peace arises in our heart.

However, believing in Him like this is not enough. We also have to do good deeds. Doing good can be all sorts of things. In the rules for believers some things are explicitly mentioned, like taking care of our parents, relatives, orphans (interestingly, Muhammad was an orphan), the needy and travelers, not killing since life is inviolable, not committing sexual offences, and so on. Goodness, honesty and solidarity are the moral message from Islam. What can also be regarded as good is the following of the five pillars of Islam: the confession of faith, the daily prayers, the annual fasting, the visiting of Mecca at least once in our life, and continually sharing our wealth with others. Everything we do well will be repaid on the big Day of Judgment. That also applies to everything we do wrong.

With this second theme (being a God-seeker and doing good deeds) something essential should be emphasized. This is that Ibrahim was a God-seeker and did good deeds without being a Jew or Christian. This is stated literally in the Koran.[45] He was the first Muslim. However, Ibrahim didn't know Muhammad because the prophet still had yet to be born. Implicitly therefore the Koran says that it is not strictly necessary to be a Muslim in the sense of someone who follows the formal rules of Muhammad, as long as we are a God-seeker and do good deeds. That is important, because a lot of non-Muslims already more or less fit that description. Unfortunately fundamentalist Muslims will not, in general, agree with this observation.

Foolish Fixations

Christianity is not the only religion that has a lot of foolish fixations. Islam knows how to play her part too. Let's start with the most conspicuous one, namely the position of the woman, and let's first of all establish again that in Paradise women have exactly the same position as men.

In the tough society of 1400 years ago it was Muhammad's intention to protect women, for instance, by advising her to wear a headscarf as a sign that she is not free to be had and should be left alone in the streets. Moreover, he stated that men had to care for women. That men got preferential treatment in financial affairs is probably because 1400 years ago they were the breadwinners most of the time. However, all these good intentions of Muhammad have developed in a direction that he as the messenger of Allah didn't mean.

In some countries the protection of the women has evolved to a very oppressive character. Think of the incident in a Saudi Arabian state school in spring 2002. Girls and boys were strictly separated. The girls were in a closed part of the school. A fire broke out, but the 60-year-old (and not very virile) guard was gone. He was the only one who had the key to the exit. The fire brigade arrived, but was stopped by the religious police. When they tried to save the girls anyway, they were even beaten by the "Committee for the Advancement of Good Manners and for the Prevention of Vice," as the religious police are officially called. The reason for their aggression was that the religious police were of the opinion that the girls were not decently dressed. They were not wearing the prescribed long black dress and headscarf. Fourteen girls died and fifty-two girls were wounded.[46]

In Spain an Imam was punished for including in his book a section in which there is advice on how a man can beat his wife without leaving any traces: that is, by smacking the wife with a thin stick on her hands and feet. In this way there wouldn't be any extravasations of blood.[47]

And then there is female circumcision. Those who still apply this, and there are quite a number of them, give the impression that Allah wants it. However, the obligation is nowhere stated in the Koran. The clergy who know that, but who are in favor of circumcision, say that Muhammad didn't explicitly prohibit it and it is therefore allowed. Or, what to think of the following reasoning, which is seriously put forward? Circumcision is supposed to be necessary because the heat of the climate makes women want sex more than is good for them. Circumcision brings the desire for sex back to "normal" proportions. In this reasoning, European women don't have to be circumcised, because the climate in Europe is much cooler and therefore the blood is much thicker. They already have a normal level of sexual desire.

From these and other examples emerges an image of little respect for women. If that respect were there, headscarves for her protection wouldn't be necessary any more. A greater respect for women would give them a more important position in society, which would also be good for the economic development of the country. It has been argued that when we limit the freedom of movement for half the population we would also only be able to realize half of the potential production in the economy. That may seem an extreme statement, but it is a fact that in general there is only a very poor level of economic progress in the Islamic world, and this situation can partly be attributed to the exclusion of women from being productive.

A more equal position between men and women in a society is of course detrimental to the position of Muslim men. And yet in the long run there almost seems no other alternative. In Western Europe it also took a long time before more equality arose. For example, women's suffrage dates only from the beginning of the twentieth century! And it was only after the Second World War that the emancipation of women really started. And when we take a close look, even in the Western world there still is unequal pay for equal work.

Morocco is a clear example of what can be different in the Islamic world. In 2004 a new family law was introduced. Now men and women have an equal position within their marriage. A woman is free in her choice of a man and is also allowed to divorce her husband if she wants to. To give one's daughter to someone in marriage is now only possible when the daughter agrees.[48]

One of the silliest fixations could be found in Afghanistan during the regime of the Taliban, which ended in 2001. What made it so foolish can also be found with very strict religious forms of Christianity and Judaism: the ban on having fun. At first in Afghanistan it was proclaimed evil to have a woman perform as singer, but since no one really protested against this the ban was extended more and more. People were not allowed to go to the cinema or to listen to music and dancing was prohibited. Even children's playgrounds were closed. When videos and televisions were prohibited too, people buried their electronic equipment in agricultural plastic sheeting.[49] The ban on dancing still exists in other Islamic countries like Iran.

I do not know of a single NDE in which having fun is prohibited. On the contrary, a part of being good to others is to have fun and to enjoy together whatever there is to enjoy (by the way, enjoying may also be done individually). Moreover, during NDEs beautiful music is often heard and it has been reported that there is a lot of humor in the contacts with The Light and the beings of light. Often NDEers say that The Light has a tremendous sense of humor. Some even say that laughter is an expression of God.

And Finally, the Foolish Fixation That Suicide Attacks Will Please Allah

The most striking ones are the more than one hundred suicide attacks that have taken place since the start of the Intifada in Israel and the Palestinian territory, the 9/11 attacks in 2001 in the United States, the attacks on trains in Madrid in 2004, the attacks in London in 2005, the more recent attacks in Bali, Pakistan, and India, and the list goes on and on. The reasons for the suicide attacks are diverse, but many have their direct or indirect origin in the lingering conflict in the Middle East. With this we found common ground with the foolish fixations of Judaism, as described in chapter 5.

The systematic disparaging and oppression of Palestinians by the Israelis has led to a population that has lost any hope for a better future. Here are some of the reasons for this: the economic disruption in the

Palestinian territories, the inhuman hygienic and medical situation there, the lack of future prospects, the general lack of self-respect, and the loss of honor for Palestinian men because they were beaten by Israeli soldiers in front of their family or because they were made to undress in public or because they couldn't prevent Israeli soldiers from storming into the women's quarters. All of this has led to completely traumatized people. And those kind of people do strange things and in this case even terrible things such as suicide attacks.

The reason why this kind of suicide attacks should be qualified as foolish fixations is that it is maintained that Allah approves of it. Just as in Christianity Islam has a tradition of martyrdom. When we die for God or Allah (of course in the end that is the same) then our reward will be great. That is why it is often said that the people who commit suicide are soldiers who offer themselves to Allah for the struggle against the threats against Islam, the jihad. The prospect of seventy-two virgins, who are waiting in Paradise for the suicides, are sometimes held out to them as a reward.

The holy war that gives soldiers an automatic admission to heaven has already been discussed as among one of the foolish fixations of Christianity: the Crusades. Just as in chapter 6 one can ask the question where people think they get the authorization to proclaim a holy war and to determine for God that He has to admit the warriors of their war to his Paradise. The comparison with the crusades is even broader. Just as in the time of the Crusades, children are also used now, and sometimes without them knowing it! In March 2004 a small 12-year-old child was stopped at the checkpoint between Nablus and Jerusalem with a ten-kilo bomb in his rucksack. The Israelis said that the child worked as a porter at the checkpoint and for that reason he didn't know he was carrying a bomb. The detonator could be set off from a distance with a mobile phone. This was different from a child that in the same month carried a bomb under his clothes. He couldn't say that he didn't know this.

Women are also deployed.[50] In 2004 in an Israeli and Palestinian television broadcast the smirking sheik Ahmed Yassin (who was shot out of his wheelchair by an Israeli rocket just a few months later) said that the first female Hamas suicide attack was one of a high-quality. The woman who did it left two children behind, one less than two years old and the other three years old. Why? Was it voluntary or had she been forced? It was argued that some of the female suicides acted to save the family's good name that they had allegedly besmirched. If they hadn't carried out the suicide attack, their family would have killed them anyway.

Suppose it is true that during their life review in the presence of The Light, the people who commit suicide get to see and feel in the greatest detail the immeasurable sorrow and pain they inflicted on others (as if it were caused to themselves). This might serve to act as an immeasurable punishment. Similarly, the people who incited others to undertake these terrorist attacks will probably have to feel the pain and sorrow of all the victims and their surviving relatives in addition to the pain and sorrow of the person who committed the suicide attack. Suicide and murder are not beneficial things to do. Urging people to do these things is probably worse. The people that do this have hugely failed their own major jihad (according to Mohammad the major jihad is our inner struggle against our own self-centeredness).

Suicide attacks inspired by religion are foolish to say the least, but the idea that martyrdom can be achieved by suicide is even more foolish. Take for instance the war between Iraq and Iran. Already forgotten this? How quickly time passes. The war started in 1980 when Sadam Hussein had his army occupy a few islands in the river on the boundary between the two countries. The war lasted for eight years. An incredible number of people lost their lives in this war—more than one million! In itself this is already one of the most deplorable lows of the 20th century, but it got lower. On the Iranian side, with the foreknowledge of the highest Iranian religious leader Imam Khomeini, children were used to clear minefields. Two birds killed with one stone: the Iranian army would be able to advance without casualties and the children would go straight to Paradise, as was promised to their parents. Foolish? Absolutely.

Summary:
Putting the "Elephant" Together

We have covered five mainstream versions of the major World religions. Essential aspects of these religions were determined and occasionally they were compared with each other. In this way we are a bit more advanced than the blind men in the folk story from India, who could each feel just one side of an elephant and couldn't get the whole picture. In this chapter we will go a bit further in putting the "elephant" together and try to get a more integrated picture of what lies behind all the religions. This is what the blind men should have done: sit together and combine their tactical observations of the elephant so that they would get a more complete idea of the truth.

Nevertheless, I think it is still extremely difficult to find the real truth because we remain constrained by our limiting four space-time dimensional world. The real world most likely has many more dimensions. Therefore, we see only a small fraction of reality. The idea that more dimensions exist than the four we currently see is something that some Nobel-prize winning scientists are seriously considering.

In putting the elephant together, I will start from the essences of the NDEs and indicate which religions are in accordance with them. For a schematic overview of the parallels between the NDEs and each of the five religions I refer to table 1. In the table it is also indicated where in this book one can find something more about that particular subject.

God or The Light Is Indescribable

The first parallel between the religions and the NDEs was mentioned in the introduction to this book: we cannot imagine what that other world looks like. People who have had an NDE have a lot of trouble describing what they have seen. That applies to The Light in particular, which is full of unconditional love and has a tremendous forgiveness. NDEers are convinced that their experience is a reality and not just some sort of dream. Many even say that it is more real than what we see here on Earth. And yet they cannot possibly give a good description.

With the exception of Christianity, this is also what all religions say: don't depict God, because it is bound to fail. In Christianity (especially in Roman Catholicism) God is always depicted as an old man with a grey beard. But He cannot really be depicted. Any image of Him is inadequate. Reference to God with "He" and "Him" is already inadequate.

In Hinduism and Islam it is permissible to describe Brahman and Allah with words. For those descriptions only beautiful words may be used and so they do: they wear themselves out with dozens of wonderful descriptions.

God or The Light Seems to Be in All of Us

The only religion that frankly states that God is in all of us is Hinduism. Everyone has a piece of Brahman in him and for that reason the Hindus join their hands when greeting each other. Although Buddhists don't believe in the existence of One universal God outside of us, they do believe that we all belong to One Big Whole. These ideas correspond with what is regularly described in NDEs. We are all a part of one big whole, which I call Unity Universe. We all are a little part of God. In all of us there is a small part of The Light. Each of us is a grain of sand on the beach and God is the whole beach.

Since we all are a small part of God, we all are equally valuable and we all deserve respect. Each human is courageous because he has decided to come to Earth to learn and to develop himself or herself further.[1] The necessity of having respect for other people is an essential aspect in each of the five religions. We should be happy about that, but unfortunately it is also the case that each of these religions curtail the idea of universal respect and find ways to look down on certain people.

Although in Hinduism it is believed that we all have a part of Brahman within us (the Atman) and we therefore all deserve respect, we are not all equal. Some people deserve more respect than others. The reason for this is that they supposedly have performed better in their previous lives. Therefore, they get a better position in this life. The caste system is a horrible formalization of this idea of inequality among all parts of Brahman in all people.

In Judaism inequality arises as YHWH has given a privileged position to the Jewish people. He is supposed to have promised even a piece of land. Some Israelites used this promise to take the land from their Palestinian fellow men during a struggle that lasted for decades and unfortunately still continues till this day.

Christians introduce inequality between people when they say that we can only go to heaven when we belong to the group of chosen ones. In the broadest sense these are all the people who believe that Jesus Christ is a God and who are also baptized in his name. Until recently in the Roman Catholic Church it meant that if you were to die as a baby and hadn't been baptized, you'd unfortunately proceed straight to "limbus," an environment in between heaven and hell.

Muslims also restrict the entry to Paradise. Only people who have converted to Islam and who also have done good deeds may go there. All others will burn and drink a boiling hellish fluid for eternity.

With respect to equality, Buddhism is the one religion that is the kindest to everyone. And yet Buddhism too stresses the differences among people. Only a very limited number of people can develop quickly thanks to the Buddhist instructions and they would be able to permanently go to Nirvana. Others don't know the Buddhist instructions or don't follow them sufficiently well. They will not be able to shut off their "self" during this human life and are bound to return to Earth. A next chance may only occur after many "eons."

Love Others and Have Compassion

When we see that all religions make a distinction between people, it is all the more astonishing that they all prescribe compassion. From all NDEs it can clearly be seen that compassion and unconditional love for other people is by far the most important thing in the whole world. We can't ignore that. Love for other people, for nature, and for everything that exists, seems to be the only thing that matters. It seems as if love is the universal building block not only of the other world but probably also of ours. The more love we can show here, the greater we will be over there. But the greater we will also be here (without being able to see it ourselves).

The best thing to do is to develop compassion. We don't do that by being preoccupied with ourselves. We can only grow compassion by interacting with other people and with nature. And according to many NDEers, the best possibilities for growth don't occur when everything, both materially and emotionally, goes well for us. In that situation there would only be a limited possibility for us to practice compassion. When all goes well we don't have to change a lot and we can't make a lot of choices. However, it is very important that we use our free will to create positive ripples. By making positive choices we can demonstrate how much compassion we have. That is why the best environment to develop compassion is an environment where things don't run smoothly. Our world with all our "ups and downs" seems to be built for that purpose. It gives us a lot of possibilities to make choices.

In Hinduism compassion for others and for nature is a part of the right way (dharma). In Buddhism, through the four noble truths, compassion is shown as an indispensable part of the eightfold path. In Judaism to love others as ourselves is an explicit order. In Christianity Jesus combined this commandment with the commandment to love God. In this way He equated the love for God with the love for our fellow man and ourselves. And in Islam it is stated that it is impossible for Muslims to enter Paradise when they haven't been good to others.

A special form of compassion is when we are happy for the lives of other people (and animals). However difficult others may act toward us (and some people can really drive us crazy), they give us the possibility to learn. I am aware that that this may sound far-fetched, but this is what I understand from NDEers. The consequence of such a form of compassion is that we don't kill others. In NDEs killing is considered to be far from the best way of behavior; we shouldn't do it and we aren't allowed to do it. Committing suicide is included within this definition, because it is a special form of killing. By killing someone or committing suicide we show the opposite of love. We move away from love and thus distance ourselves from The Light. For this reason it may not really come as a surprise that all religions warn against killing. In both Hinduism and Buddhism killing and suicide stain our karma and in one of our next lives we will, in one or other way, get it back. In Judaism and the two religions of Islam and Christianity derived from Judaism, the act of killing is even explicitly prohibited.

Everyone Has His Own Task

The only religion that pays a significant amount of attention to the task everyone has in this life is Hinduism. We have to perform our task as well as we possibly can. Our task and the dedicated performance of it are the most important themes of that religion. This is also what a lot of NDEers discover when they are almost dead. Many state that every human has a specific task.[2] It may be a task tailored to that individual and which has to be performed during that individual's life. During the NDE there may have been some communication about this task or the contents of it may have been made clear in another way. A few NDEers can still remember exactly what their task is. It may, for instance, have something to do with their private life, like the caring for children, but the task may also relate to something more social. For example, one mentioned the individual contribution of people to the opening up of the American continent in the 18th and 19th centuries.[3]

After their return, however, most NDEers do not remember their task anymore. During their experience it has sometimes been explicitly communicated to them, but during their return they just cannot hold onto what it is. They know they are expected to do something, but they simply forgot what that was. It is completely gone and whatever they try to do to remember it, it just doesn't come back to them.

All NDEers have the strong feeling that each human life is valuable. They feel there is no individual on Earth whose life is meaningless. People who we may think are utterly unimportant still have a life that is meaningful in a way that we cannot understand on Earth. This applies also to the beggar or the drunk in the street.[4] NDEers often state that with our limited view of reality we aren't able to see how important their lives are. It could even be that the lives of those people are in one way or another important for the fulfillment of the task in our own life.

Although the individual task is central to Hinduism, it seems that the way it is interpreted does not correspond to the things NDEers say about it. The tasks that everyone has in Hinduism are laid down in a very detailed way in the caste system. The task is a function of one's social position. The impression I get from NDEs is that this representation is too simplistic. Our tasks do not have to be related to our social position at all. If you are a priest, your task could be to lead a spiritual life and to be an example to others, but it could just as well be that your primary task is something completely different. For instance, it might have to do with the way in which you structure your relationship with your parents, your children, or your neighbor.

Apart from Hinduism, Judaism is the only other major religion in which something is said about a task and the way in which that task should be performed. It has clear parallels with what many NDEers say. Although in Judaism there is no explicit mention of an individual task, it is stated that we all have the task to contribute to creation. YHWH completed his work in six days and now it is our turn to continue that work. The purpose is to establish the kingdom of YHWH. What that means or how it should eventually look remains unclear. We work on something, but we don't know what we're working on, and thus we also don't know exactly what we have to do. This latter point corresponds with what NDEers say.

We all have to do something, which will eventually lead to a result that in one way or another is of great importance. In the meanwhile we will experience all kinds of setbacks and misfortunes. This is recognized in Judaism, but a reason for it is not given. We will not be able to understand what the purpose is that YHWH has for us by giving us setbacks and misfortunes. That simply is too complicated for us. The only thing that we can do is just to go on with our life. We have to believe that He/She has a good reason for everything. In any case, misery and problems are not meant to be a punishment. This is also very much in agreement with what NDEers say.

Punishment

Misery, pain, sorrow, and all kinds of setbacks don't exist to thwart us. The Light doesn't take pleasure in hurting people. It doesn't enjoy it when we suffer pain, are hungry, unwell, or when a misfortune strikes us. Although some people insist otherwise, it is not the case that misery and setbacks exist as a kind of punishment for what we did wrong previously. Hurricane Katrina and subsequently Hurricane Rita, are not a punishment from God, nor are earthquakes or tsunamis. The Light, or God, or however we want to refer to It, doesn't punish. Manmade misery and failures should also not be considered as a punishment from God. The worst example of this is war. According to an NDEer who explicitly asked about it, war is not what God wants.[5] He doesn't like it. That it happens anyway, or that He allows it to occur, is because it is the result of the free will of people. When enough people desire it, war can take place, but God still doesn't like it. It is against God's or The Light's nature, because Its nature is one of unconditional love.

The only reason why problems occur is to give us the opportunity to make choices. The more choices we have, the more opportunities exist for us to develop compassion for people.[6] Of course our choices do not always lead us to a solution to our problem and indeed sometimes there is no solution at all to a specific problem, but it is not about reaching a solution at all. It is about the way in which we deal with the problem; it is about our reaction to the problem. In particular it is about the intentions we have.

The life review that is sometimes described in NDEs should not be seen as a punishment either. It seems not to be intended as a punishment because even during the review, when we feel in great detail what we did to others and are deeply ashamed of it, The Light remains loving, forgiving, and full of compassion. In not one case did The Light become angry. Never did it stamp its feet with rage nor did it point at rules from any particular religion.

Judaism is the only religion that doesn't explicitly hold out the prospect of punishments when we don't behave in a prescribed way. Christianity and Islam, however, are full admonitions and we are continuously threatened with an eternal stay in hell. In Hinduism and Buddhism we seem to be confronted through our karma with our evil deeds from previous lives. That can be interpreted as a kind of punishment, but it can also be regarded as a possibility to neutralize and to correct loveless decisions from a previous life. This does require, however, that everything each of us has done is remembered. This applies to the numerous acts and thoughts of the billions of people on the Earth.

All You Have Done Is Remembered

It is unbelievable, but from NDEs it turns out that everything including the smallest detail is recorded. It is all still there. Everything we have done, said, and thought (as well as everything we haven't done, said, or thought) is shown to us again during our life review.

All religions mention the recording of everything we have done. In Hinduism and Buddhism everything is kept in our karma. And in the three other religions everything is remembered by YHWH, God, and Allah, and is shown to us on the Day of Judgment. Moreover, in Buddhism, Judaism, and Christianity it is explicitly stated that not only our deeds will be remembered, but also that our thoughts are of great importance and will therefore be recorded.

Is There a Heaven; Is There a Hell?

And now the big question: will we all go to heaven? From NDEs it doesn't appear that anyone is excluded. More than that, in principle everyone can go to heaven, which is the place where the loving Light is. It doesn't matter what religion you adhere to and even atheists aren't excluded. What does seem to happen is that some people can be stuck between what we call Heaven and Earth. The reason for that is certainly not clear yet. A possible explanation could be that they are still too much attached to Earth. This could be a consequence of too much attachment to physical things or to an addiction, or just because they feel they still have to exert an influence over something. It could also be that they want to say sorry for committing suicide or that they are still too preoccupied with themselves. In the latter case their ego is the only thing they see, which means they do not yet have an eye for The Light. In a sense they are blinded by their own ego. The lack of love for others blocks their view on the love outside of themselves.

Sometimes, however, real hell-like environments have been reported, and I mean dreary and even scary environments with hostile and aggressive creatures. Fortunately, the people concerned (or rather their spirits) are not left to fend for themselves. Beings of light would be in their immediate vicinity, ready to help the moment it becomes possible. That seems to be easier when the spirits concerned are open for love and ask for it.[7] There might be an easy explanation for this. Since we all are part of The Light, we are essentially attracted towards It. This makes a full and definitive separation from The Light unthinkable.

While according to NDEers, there seems to be no hindrance to one's entry into heaven, all the mainstream religions speak about clear limitations. In Hinduism entry into heaven is possible, but only after a very long and arduous period of training that involves intensive meditation. An alternative is that we fulfill our duty meticulously while dedicating the fruit of it to Brahman. In Buddhism it is also possible to permanently break away from rebirth and enter the nirvana. That, however, is not at all easy because it requires us to discard the "self," which is only possible after eons of training. In Judaism it is possible for everyone to go to heaven, including for those who don't adhere to the Jewish belief. The only impediment is when we have done wrong. Then we have to remain in hell for a specific period of time. Although this would not be fun, it is much better than in Christianity or Islam. There they believe in significant hindrances to one's entry to heaven. It is only possible to go to heaven when we were good, but we also have to be Christian or Muslim, respectively. Anyone who doesn't meet these requirements goes to hell for eternity. To be perfectly clear: hell doesn't only exist solely in these three mainstream religions; it also exists in Hinduism and Buddhism.

Attachment to Matter

From reports of NDEers it appears time and again that the attachment to matter is not really optimal. Material things are just not important. When people die, they are glad that they don't "wear" that body anymore. In fact they are extremely happy to be released from that matter. That is to say, this is when they have had a blissful NDE.

There are people who cannot give up matter after their death. Too much attachment to matter confines us to Earth when we die. Those are the people who cannot break free from Earth and therefore seem to have difficulty proceeding towards The Light. Here we find a parallel with all religions. In each of them it more or less appears that attachment to matter is wrong and hinders our ascent to heaven. This is most clear in Hinduism and Buddhism, but in Christianity it is also expressly stated when Jesus says that rich people will have more trouble going to heaven. He says that a camel has fewer problems passing through the eye of a needle than a wealthy person passing on to heaven.

There Is Free Will

From NDEs the existence of a free will clearly emerges.[8] And yet there still is a kind of dilemma. There is a free will, but everyone also has a task to fulfill. You don't have a choice in this.

Of all the religions the concept of free will seems to be most prominent in Judaism. Under all circumstances you can choose because through free will you can show how good you are. Especially when things are against you it is important to choose the right way. This means that you have to do beneficial things. Not only is doing well of great importance. Having good thoughts is important too. In fact, NDEers say that good intentions are of the greatest importance. When your intentions are good (meaning what you had "in mind"), but the result leaves a lot to be desired, your good intentions still count.

Christianity and Islam struggle the most with the concept of free will. On the one hand it is recognized that every human has a free will, but on the other hand God or Allah seem to fix a lot of things. In Christianity, for instance, who goes to heaven is already determined. In Islam Allah has established himself on his throne, from where He governs the universe in great detail.

Reincarnation

Reincarnation is an essential aspect of Hinduism and Buddhism, but not of the other three religions. A significant number of NDEers do not rule out reincarnation and after their experience, many of them even started to believe in it. During their experience some even see spirits or beings of light who, with enthusiasm, are ready to incarnate on Earth as a baby.[9] This, however, doesn't have to mean that all those spirits were human beings before. It could very well be that spirits go to Earth only once and do not return after their death. However, those that do believe in reincarnation, usually point out specific cases where people remember parts of their previous lives. In a number of these cases situations were described that could even be verified to have existed.

This could mean that we may have to conclude that reincarnation really exists. In that case there would be all the more reason to be good to everyone, to ensure that everyone has enough to eat and drink, and to protect nature. If reincarnation exists, then perhaps we will be reborn as a poor child in our next life in one of the gigantic slums of one of the many mega cities in a developing country. Should reincarnation exist, then perhaps in the next life we will be at the mercy of someone we treated badly in this life. And should reincarnation exist, we will return to an environment that we helped to pollute, and therefore has less forests, and a shortage of clean water, and a smaller variety of plants and animals.

Reincarnation is difficult to prove and is therefore a very difficult subject. Even when people say that they can remember a previous life and the details discussed can also be verified, it doesn't mean that reincarnation really exists. It could also be that such a person can remember an identity of someone who lived before, while not having been that person.[10]

In order to clarify what I mean about the difficulty of the subject of reincarnation, I refer back to the father who explains to his son how he has to interpret the equality between his own soul (the Atman) and God (Brahman; see chapter 3). The father asks his son to put salt in a bowl of water and to come back tomorrow. The salt, of course, dissolves in the water. He uses this example to show that the essence of Brahman is everywhere. The story of the father and the son ends here, but I want to extend it as follows.

The dissolved salt in the water is Brahman. Suppose the bowl is really very big; suppose it is the ocean and we can draw many billions of cups of water from it with each cup representing a human. When a human dies his cup of water is tossed back into the ocean again. When a baby is born, a new cup of water is drawn. The chance is extremely small that exactly the same salt molecules that had been in a previous cup again end up in a new cup. There might be a few of those molecules in the new cup and maybe that is already sufficient to remember a previous life. It may even be possible that we don't even need a molecule of a previous cup to remember a previous life. In this case we enter into the field of a collective subconsciousness: your memories are then partly accessible to me (and the other way round).

I don't mean that reincarnation is possible or impossible, but with this example I merely want to indicate that reincarnation is easy to theorize about but difficult to prove.

Get Aligned with The Light

Until now religions have told us that they have the answers to many, if not all of the spiritual questions we may have with respect to the purpose of our life, the way we have to live it, and what happens to us after we die. Over the course of time they have claimed a monopoly on the answers to these matters and have even engaged in some fierce competition with each other. Fortunately, through NDEers we got an alternative view on all these sorts of spiritual questions. Through them we know that the search for answers is not over yet and still continues.

When we add all the essences together of the summaries of the different religions that I have discussed, we in fact make a start in assembling the elephant, just like the blind men could have done in the Indian folk story. The result closely resembles NDEs. Therefore, my principal conclusion is that the essences of the religions can be found in NDEs, but not all essences of the NDEs can be found again in each of the religions. Consequently, NDEs are more universal than each of the religions separately.

To demonstrate how unnecessary the bitter competition among the religions is and that no one religion can claim to hold the all-embracing truth, I would like to quote some NDEers. One said that no one pure religion exists, but that The Light values all churches and religions and finds them important.[11] This seems to indicate that The Light has provided for a large supply of religions so that people can chose the best religion for their spiritual growth. Another NDEer said that what struck her is that it does not matter how we address The Light, just as long as we address Him/Her. God makes no distinction between Muslim, Christian, Jewish, Hindu or any other kind of prayer. He/She hears them all equally.[12] Many more say similar things.

During his experience, one NDEer even asked point-blank which religion is the best.[13] The answer was as short as it was clear: "The religion that brings you closest to God." From that answer it is also clear that it does not matter which religion you believe in. This person also says: "The purpose of religion is to have a personal relationship with God. Religion is only a means to find God. Religion is not a destination.... God is far greater than any religion."[14] This NDEer also gives us a warning. He says that God abhors it when people use religion for their own purposes or to demean other people. That is one of the most terrible things we can do. I believe that this has, unfortunately, happened many times in the past, and still happens today.

Although, in my opinion it is a very important conclusion that The Light, or whatever you want to call It, is a far greater concept than is described or seen or adhered to in any of the five great religions, the most important conclusion of my search is that we all have the possibility to see The Light and to arrive in the light environment after our death. The reason is that we *are* The Light. We are part of it; It is part of us. We cannot separate ourselves from It. So in order to go back "home" we don't have to adhere to any specific religion. People who do not follow any religion at all can also make their way to this fulfilling environment. Whether after our death we will directly arrive there, seems to depend on ourselves. We shouldn't be overly selfish or too preoccupied with our ego. Attachment to material things also seems to be a hampering factor. In addition, hate and grudges seem to be serious hindrances to arriving directly in that wonderful place. The best circumstances we can create for ourselves are when we have tried to love others unconditionally. With this, our intentions seem to be extremely important. In fact, all of this implies that the more we are in alignment with The Light (of unconditional love), the better it is.

The Essences of NDEs and the Comparison with the Five Religions to Show the Parallels

Essences of NDEs	Hinduism	Buddhism
God or The Light is indescribable.	There are many descriptions of Brahman.	Nirvana is indescribable.
God or The Light seems to be in everything.	The trinity is in everyone. Atman is in everyone. Brahman is everywhere and in everything, including people and animals.	
God or The Light is present in all creatures and therefore everyone is equal.	In principle wise people see others as their equals, but there is a considerable amount of inequality due to the caste system.	
People are equal (therefore men and women are also equal).	This is because everyone has an Atman, which is a part of Brahman. Nevertheless there is great inequality because of the caste system.	
Everything is one; everything belongs to one whole; there seems to be unity in everything.	Brahman is in everything.	To some extent in nirvana.
Love others; have compassion for others.	Dharma prescribes compassion for others.	Compassion for everyone; the eightfold path.
Respect for life and nature.	This follows from being part of Brahman. Dharma prescribes it too.	See the eightfold path.
No murder and no suicide.	No murder and no suicide. Killing is bad for our karma, although Rama kills the golden deer (which is controversial), and there are many stories about wars and killing.	Implicit in the eightfold path.
Everyone has his or her own task.	Fulfill your own task, but renounce the fruit of it.	
Misfortune is not bad in principle; it is there for a specific reason.		

Judaism	Christianity	Islam
YHWH is indescribable and may, therefore, not even be depicted.		Allah is indescribable and may, therefore, not be depicted. Allah has many names or descriptions.
Eve was created as an equal to Adam and Serai was treated as equal by Abram. For Orthodox Jews, however, men have preferential treatment.	Yes, according to Jesus, although the notion of the chosen few, who will go to heaven, exists.	Men and women who are Muslim and have done good deeds will go to the same Paradise.
Love others as we would love ourselves as it is mentioned by Moses and other prophets.	The central theme of Jesus's teaching is perfect love. He refers to what Moses and the prophets say: love others as we love ourselves.	This commandment is not so very explicit as in other religions, but having respect for others is definitely thought to be important.
We may eat meat, but we have to respect the sanctity of the life of animals.		Included in the rules for believers.
We may eat meat, but not human meat. Killing is prohibited in the Ten Commandments.	According to the covenant with Noah and the Ten Commandments of Moses.	Included in the rules for believers, although killing is allowed in certain circumstances.
God started creation; we have to continue to work on it.		
There is a reason for misfortune, but we cannot understand what it is. Why should we accept fortune and not misfortune?		

ESSENCES OF NDEs	HINDUISM	BUDDHISM
No explicit punishment for bad behavior (The Light remains loving).		
The thoughts one has are important.		Included in karma.
Everything you do is registered.	Included in karma.	Included in karma.
Heaven is just around the corner; it is very near (it is not a dichotomy).	In the sense that a part of Brahman (Atman) is in all of us, heaven must be very near.	Point of quietness in ourselves.
Everyone can in principle go to heaven or paradise (or reach nirvana).	Yes, in principle, but it is very difficult and takes a lot of effort.	Yes, in principle, but it is very difficult and takes a lot of effort.
Don't get attached to matter.	Live an ascetic life.	Attachment makes us think that there is "me" and "the others."
There is free will.	Meditation, unattached action and devotion are our own responsibility, although it is pre-specified which castes can do it and when.	Trust yourself. No need to follow anyone or anything.
There is a hell or hellish environment.	People who do evil go to hell.	It is one of the six worlds of existence.
Reincarnation. Many, but not all NDEers believe there seems to be something true about reincarnation.	Based on our karma.	Based on our karma.

Judaism	Christianity	Islam
There are no punishments mentioned along with the Ten Commandments. Misfortune is no punishment; it helps us to realize God's kingdom.		
According to the Ten Commandments, good thoughts are important.	Loving thoughts are just as important as loving actions.	
On the Day of Judgment everything you have done seems to be remembered, because it will be judged.	On Judgment Day everything you have done seems to be remembered, because it will be judged.	Everything you have seen, heard, and felt is known, because questions will be asked about all of it.
There is a relationship between things happening on earth and in heaven. An example is the establishment of the kingdom by the Messiah.		Allah is very near. He is even nearer than the carotid artery and can bring peace in our heart.
Yes, you only have to love YHWH and be good to others, i.e., to love our neighbors as we love ourselves.	Yes, according to Jesus, if we show a lot of love and are not attached to matter. No, according to Augustine, because we have to be Christian to have a chance to go to heaven.	Everyone who believes and does good will go to heaven. However, in Islam believing has been equated with being a Muslim.
	Share everything with others. Rich people have more problems entering heaven.	
There is free will.	There has to be free will, although according to Augustine it does not seem to matter since it is predetermined who goes to hell.	There is free will, but Allah is also involved in everything (this has become a very complicated dogma).
There is Gehenna, where bad people will stay temporarily.	Following the Jewish belief, there is a hell. Augustine defines those who go there. One will stay there forever. Jesus mentions hell too.	There is a hell where people go who have done bad things. Also, unbelievers will go there. Once there, there is no escape.
No reincarnation.	No reincarnation.	No reincarnation.

Notes

Chapter 2

1 Rene Jorgensen, pp 5-9.
2 Taylor, p. 140.
3 Cox-Chapman, p. 80.
4 Grossman, p.63.
5 To read more about distressful NDEs, please read my previous book *Messages from The Light* or the book by Barbara Rommer titled *Blessing In Disguise: Another Side of the Near Death Experience*. People with distressful NDEs are advised to read Nancy Evans Bush's book "Dancing Past the Dark" or visit her website www.dancingpastthedark.com <http://www.dancingpastthedark.com>
6 Storm, pp. 10-18.
7 Storm, p. 101.
8 Notably in chapter 6, but in other chapters too.
9 A more extensive discussion of messages can be found in my previous book *Messages from The Light*.
10 Burrows, p.3-6.
11 Ring and Franklin, p. 206.
12 Futrell, p. 9.
13 Moody (1976), p. 44.
14 Cox-Chapman, p. 58, Opdebeeck, p. 144 en 202.

Chapter 3

1 Shattuck, p. 142-143.
2 Smith, p. 138.
3 Bowker, p. 21.
4 Shattuck, p. 22.
5 Hemenway, p. 28.
6 See for the Upanishads for instance Olivelle or Mascaró.
7 Kena Upanishad, part 4.
8 Katha Upanishad, part 5.
9 Mundaka Upanishad, part 3, chapter 1.
10 Mundaka Upanishad, part 3, chapter 2.
11 Svetasvatara Upanishad, part 2.
12 Svetasvatara Upanishad, part 4.
13 Svetasvatara Upanishad, part 5.
14 Svetasvatara Upanishad, part 6.
15 Maitri Upanishad, 6.17.
16 Taittiriya Upanishad, 3.1-6.
17 Chandogya Upanishad, 3.14.
18 Brihad-Aranyaka Upanishad, 4.3-4.
19 Mundaka Upanishad, part 3, chapter 1, Mascaró, p. 80.
20 Katha Upanishad, part 6.
21 Mundaka Upanishad, part 3, chapter 1.
22 Katha Upanishad, part 6.
23 Mundaka Upanishad, part 3, chapter 1, Mascaró, p. 80.

24 Chandogya Upanishad, 6.12-14; Mascaró, p. 117-118.
25 Cox-Chapman, p. 80.
26 Burton, p. 14.
27 Isa Upanishad.
28 Chandogya Upanishad; Mascaró, p. 120.
29 Katha Upanishad.
30 Chandogya Upanishad.
31 Katha Upanishad.
32 The Supreme Teaching (Brihad-Aranyaka Upanishad), 4.3-4, Mascaró, p. 139.
33 The Supreme Teaching (Brihad-Aranyaka Upanishad), 4.3-4, Mascaró, p. 140.
34 Opdebeeck, p. 170.
35 Katha Upanishad; Shattuck, p. 33.
36 Mandukya Upanishad.
37 Mundaka Upanishad, part 1, chapter 2.
38 Bhagavad Gita, 9:23, 10:20, 11, 13:12-18.
39 Bhagavad Gita, 2:19-22.
40 Bhagavad Gita, 2:31-33, 18:7.
41 Bhagavad Gita, 3:35.
42 Gandhi, p. 41.
43 Bhagavad Gita, 2:47-51, 18:9.
44 Bhagavad Gita, 9, Gandhi, p. 11.
45 Bhagavad Gita, 2:71, 5:19, 12:13-20, 18:20.
46 Bhagavad Gita, 11:12.
47 Bhagavad Gita, 11:15-18 and 11:37.
48 Hemenway, p. 54.
49 Vanamali, p. 21.
50 Narayan, p. 56.
51 Burton, p. 14.
52 O'Neil, pp. 2-31.
53 Lonely Planet, p. 44.

Chapter 4

1 MacQuitty, pp. 56-63.
2 MacQuitty, p. 77-80.
3 For an overview of the history of Buddhism, see Conze.
4 Dalai Lama (1997), p. 120.
5 Armstrong, p. 75-78.
6 Armstrong, p. 90.
7 Lowenstein, pp. 20-21.
8 Armstrong, p. 85.
9 Dalai Lama (1997), p. 37-38, Bowker (2000)
10 Dalai Lama (1995), p. 153-154.
11 Geshe Kelsang Gyatso, p.22, Thurman, p.50.
12 Dalai Lama (1995), p. 39 and 45.
13 Dalai Lama (1997), p. 124.
14 Dalai Lama (1997), p. 18.
15 Thurman, p. 17.
16 Thurman, p. 65.

17 Thurman, p. 253, Fremante, p. 115.
18 Dalai Lama (1997), p. 84-87.
19 Thurman, p. 70-71.
20 Sogyal Rinpoche, p. 258.
21 Thurman, p. 165-169, Fremante, p. 42-44.
22 Sogyal Rinpoche, p. 258.
23 Thurman, pp. 68-73.
24 Victoria, p. 161.
25 Victoria, p. 144
26 Victoria, p. 137.
27 Victoria, p. 13.
28 Victoria, p.145.
29 Victoria, p. 138.
30 Victoria, p. 140.

Chapter 5

1   Translations of the Jewish texts of Reisel and Fox have been used.
2   Szulk, p.96.
3   See Friedman who shows that in the Bible there are different styles of writing and he indicates this by using different colors for each of the texts.
4   Leviticus, 19:18 and 33-34.
5   Burrows, p. 6. Mrs. Burrows is busy with publishing her very extensive NDE.
6   Borrows, p. 5.
7   Deutronomy, 6:4.
8   Matthew, 22:36-40.
9   The Christian bible starts with the sentence: "In the beginning God created the heaven and the earth."
10 Genesis, 2:7
11 Epstein, p. 20.
12 Genesis, 8:21-22.
13 Genesis, 9:6.
14 Exodus 19:6.
15 Szulk, p. 106.
16 Genesis, 15:5
17 Genesis 13:16.
18 Epstein, pp. 14-15.
19 Genesis, 12:7.
20 Genesis 16.
21 Genesis 16.9.
22 Genesis 17:22.
23 Genesis 21:9-21 and 25:12-18.
24 The story of the exodus is in Exodus.
25 Exodus, 19:16-20.
26 Exodus 19:6.
27 Epstein, 21-22.
28 Fox, p. 368.
29 Fox, p. 1013.

30 Also see Storm, pp. 42 and 61.
31 Books of Wisdom, Job, 2:10
32 Proverbs 1:1-9 and 20:24.
33 The story of Sodom and Gomorrah can be found in the Torah, Genesis chapters 13, 18 and 19.
34 Genesis 13:13.
35 Genesis 19:4.
36 Tanakh, Prophets, Ezekiel 16:44-63.
37 For those who really want to continue to be condemning of homosexuality, there are still other sections in the Bible, for instance, in Leviticus, 18:22 in which it is said that you shouldn't lie with a man as with a woman because that is an abomination.
38 Burton, p. 6. See also Dale 2006 and 2007, and Corcoran.
39 Epstein, 138.
40 Tanakh, Isaiah, 56.
41 Prediker, 12:7.
42 Epstein, p. 30.
43 Isaiah, 30:33
44 Epstein, p.148.
45 Cooley, p. 32.
46 Cooley, p. 93.
47 Cockburn, p.107.
48 See for instance Leviticus 19:33-34
49 See for instance in the Torah, Leviticus, 19:33-34 or almost the same in Deuteronomy 10: 18-19.

Chapter 6

1 Jesus is supposed to have said that He is the Son of God a number of times, e.g. Matthew, 17:16, 15-17.
2 Russell, p. 368.
3 Matthew, 1:24.
4 Matthew, 12:46-50.
5 Mark, 6:3.
6 Mark, 15:40.
7 Storm, p. 34.
8 Burton, p. 6.
9 Russell, pp. 358-366, 452-463.
10 Russell, pp. 364-366.
11 John, 3:5.
12 Matthew, 22:14.
13 John, 1:29.
14 Romans, 5:12-21.
15 Matthew, 11:14 and 17:10-13, and Mark, 9-12.
16 John, 3:6-7.
17 Matthew, 9:18-26, Mark 5:21-43, Luke 8:40-56.
18 Matthew, 14:13-21, Mark 6:30-44, Luke, 9:10-17, John, 6:1-15 and the second one in Matthew, 15 29-39, Mark, 8:1-10.
19 Matthew, 5:17-19.
20 Matthew, 22:36-40, and Mark, 12:28-31, Luke, 10:25-28.
21 Mark, 12:28-34.

22 Matthew, 5:39.
23 Luke, 6:27-36.
24 Matthew, 5:44-45.
25 Luke 7:47.
26 Matthew, 19:28.
27 John 5:22 and 27.
28 Matthew, 7:1.
29 Matthew, 18:21-22.
30 Matthew, 7:12.
31 Matthew, 25:40.
32 Matthew, 19:16-24, Mark, 10:17-27, Luke, 18:18-24.
33 Mark, 10:43-45.
34 Suleman, p. 28, Storm, pp. 52-54, 59, 73.
35 Mark Giordani, p. 5.
36 Ritchie, p. 47-67.
37 Storm, pp. 19-29.
38 Matthew, 7:21.
39 Luke, 16:25-26.
40 Luke, 6:35.
41 Schouten; also go and see the witches' weighing house in Oudewater, the Netherlands.
42 Michelin, New England, p. 142.
43 Duffy, p.105.
44 Duffy, p.115.
45 Russell, pp. 434-435.
46 Russell, p. 442.
47 Gaykrant (a Dutch gay magazine) 22 November to 5 December 2003, p.23.

Chapter 7

1 When referring to verses (Suras) in the Koran the count of the Royal Egyptian Koran Edition from 1924 is used.
2 Attema, pp. 69-70 [and 75-76].
3 Sura 17:110, 59:24.
4 Sura 42:9.
5 Sura 43:4.
6 Sura 5:44 and 46.
7 Attema, p. 11 [12].
8 Attema, p. 41.
9 Ritchie, pp. 66-67.
10 Sura 11:61, 20:55, 71:18
11 Sura 7:80-81, 29:28-30.
12 This is described in Sura 22:78.
13 Sura 17:22-39.
14 Sura 17:9-11
15 Kramers, p.5.
16 Sura 26:19.
17 Ritchie, pp. 66-67 and Storm.
18 Attema, p.42.
19 Sura 6:12.
20 Sura 27:11.

21 Sura 61:4.
22 Sura 13:6 and 4:22.
23 Sura 23:16, 45:26.
24 Sura 31:33, 34:37, 70:10, 82:19.
25 Sura 39:70.
26 Sura 58:7, 60:3.
27 Sura 41:20-22.
28 Sura 6:130.
29 Sura 99:7-8. See also Sura 40:40.
30 Sura 67:3.
31 Suras 33:35 and 40:40.
32 Suras 13:35, 35:33-36, 36:11-40, 47:15, 54:54, 55:46-61 and 76:5-22.
33 Suras 15:46-47 and 35:34-35.
34 Suras 37:40-49, 56:11-40, 76:5-22.
35 See also Attema, p. 58.
36 Sura 15:43-44.
37 Suras 4:56, 22:19-20, 25:12, 67:6-12, 69:32, 70:15, 73:12, 74:27, 84:12 and 90:20.
38 Suras 14:16, 18:29, 37:65-67, 47:15, 73:13 and 78:24-25.
39 Sura 2:80.
40 Ritchie, pp. 66-67.
41 Suras 17:13-15, 57:22 and 65:3.
42 Sura 2:253.
43 Könemann, p. 98.
44 Sura 50:16.
45 Suras 2:140 and 3:67.
46 NRC (Dutch newspaper), Friday, March 15, 2002.
47 NRC (Dutch newspaper), Thursday, January 15, 2004.
48 NRC (Dutch newspaper), Tuesday, February 10, 2004.
49 NRC (Dutch newspaper), month edition September 2003.
50 NRC (Dutch newspaper), Thursday, January 15, 2004.

Chapter 8

1 Eadie, p. 55.
2 Suleman, p. 19.
3 Eadie, p. 58.
4 Eadie, p. 101-104.
5 Storm, pp. 38-41.
6 Suleman, p. 21.
7 Ritchie, pp. 66-67.
8 Storm, 41, 53-54, 63, 78-80; Eadie, pp. 56, 103, 108.
9 Eadie, pp. 93-99.
10 See for instance Eadie, p. 96.
11 Eadie, p. 53.
12 Suleman, p. 54.
13 Storm, p. 73.
14 Storm, p. 73.

References and Bibliography

Armstrong, Karen. *Buddha*. New York: Penguin Books, 2001.

Attema, D.S. *De Koran, Zijn ontstaan en inhoud*. 3rd ed. Kampen: Kok, 1993.

Bowker, J. *The Concise Oxford Dictionary of World Religions*. Oxford: Oxford University Press.

Burrows, Bonni J. "My Journey through a Doorway called Death." *Vital Signs*, Vol. XXIV, No. 1, 3-6, 2005.

Burton, Catherine. "Counselling from a Near-Death Perspective." *Vital Signs*, Vol. XXI No. 4 and XXII No. 1, 2002/2003, pp. 5-15.

Bush, Nancy Evans. *Dancing Past the Dark: Distressing Near-Death Experiences*. Nancy Evans Bush Publishing, 2012.

Cockburn, Andrew. "Lines in the Sand. Deadly Times in the West Bank and Gaza." *National Geographic*, October 2002, pp. 102-111.

Conze, Edward. *Buddhism: A Short History*. London: One World Publications.

Cooley, John K. *Green March, Black September: The Story of the Palestinian Arabs*. London: Frank Cass, 1973.

Coppes, Christophor. Messages *From the Light: True Stories of Near-Death Experiences and Communication from the Other Side*. Pompton Plains, N.J.: New Page Books, N.J., 2011.

Corcoran, Diane. *When Ego Dies: A Compilation of Near-Death & Mystical Conversion Experiences*. Hot Spring National Park, Ark.: Emerald Ink Publishing, 1996.

Cox-Chapman, Mally. *Glimp van de hemel. Bewijzen voor een leven na de dood*, Ankh-Hermes, Deventer, 1996 (original title: *The Case for Heaven*. New York: G. P. Putnam's Sons, 1995.

Dalai Lama. *De kracht van het mededogen*. Rainbow Pocketboeken, Uitgeverij BZZTôH, Den Haag, 1995. (original title: *The Power of Compassion*, 1995).

Dalai Lama. *Leven in Vrede, sterven in vrede*. The library of Tibet, 1997. (original title: *The Joy of Living and Dying in Peace*. New York: Harper Collins, 1997.)

Dale, Liz. "From Fear to Love in Gay and Lesbian Near-Death Experiences and the Coming out Process." *Journal of Near-Death Studies*, Vol. 25, 2006, nr. 3, 171-179.

Dale, Liz. "Experiences of Light in Gay and Lesbian Near-Death Experiences." *Journal of Near-Death Studies*, Vol. 24, 2007, nr. 3, pp. 175-178.

Duffy, Eamon. *Heiligen & zondaars. Een geschiedenis van de pausen*. Ten Have, Baarn and Lannoo, Tielt, 1997; Original title: *Saints and Sinners: A history of the Popes*. London: Yale University Press.

Eadie, Betty J. *Geleid door het licht,* 3rd ed. A.W. Bruna Uitgevers B.V., Utrecht, 1994. (original title: *Embraced by the Light.* Placerville, California: Gold Leaf Press.

Epstein, Isidore. (original publication of 1959), *Het Jodendom, Het Spectrum.* 2nd ed. (Original title: *Judaism. A Historical Presentation,* London: Penguin Books, 1956.

Fox, Everett, trans. *The Five Books of Moses, Genesis: Exodus, Leviticus, Numbers, Deuteronomy.* New York: Schocken Books.

Fremante, Francesca, and Chögyam Trungpa, trans. (translators and commentators), *Het Tibetaans Dodenboek: De grote bevrijding door horen in de bardo,* Servire Uitgevers B.V., Cothen 1995 (English title: *The Tibetan Book of the* Dead: *The Great Liberation through Hearing in the Bardo.* Boston: Shambhala Publications, 1987).

Friedman, Richard Elliott. *The Bible with Sources Revealed: A New View Into the Five Books of Moses.* San Francisco: Harper and New York: HarperCollins Publishers, 2003.

Futrell, Michellenea. "Not Afraid of Death—But Not Allowed to Die." *Vital Signs,* Vol. 22, no. 2, 3 and 8-9.

Gandhi, Mohandas K. (Mahatma). *Bhagavad-Gítá:* commentary by Mahatma Gandhi. Axiom Publishing, 2003.

Geshe Kelsang Gyatso. *Introductie tot het Boeddhisme. Een verklaring van de Boeddhistische levenswijze.* Karuna, Tilburg (original title: *Introduction to Buddhism.* London: Tarpa Publications, 1998).

Giordani, Mark. "Mark Giordani's Journey." *Vital Signs,* IANDS, Volume XXI, No. 2, 5-18, 2002.

Grossman, Neal, Fall 2001, Forgiveness and the Near-Death Experience, Journal of Near-Death Studies, Vol. 20, no. 1, 62-62.

Hemenway, Priya. *Hindu Gods.* San Francisco: Chronicle Books, 2003.

Jorgensen, Rene. "Awakening after Life. A Firsthand Guide through Death into the Purpose of Life." www.booksurge.com, 2007.

Könemann, *Wereldreligies.* Könemann Verlagsgesellschaft mbH, Keulen, 2007.

Kramers, J.H., trans, *The Koran,* 2nd ed., edited by A. Jaber and J.J.G. Jansen, The Netherlands: De Arbeiderspers, 1997.

Lonely Planet (Monique Choy and Sarina Singh) Rajasthan, Footscray, Victoria, Australia: Lonely Planet Publications Pty Ltd, 2002.

Lowenstein, Tom. Boeddhisme, filosofie en meditatie, het pad naar spirituele verlichting, heilige plekken. Librero Nederland B.V., Kerkdriel, 2002 (original title: *The Vision of the Buddha.* Duncan Baird Publishers, 1997).

MacQuitty, William. *Boeddha.* Teleboek N.V., Bussum (original title: *Buddha*).

Mascaró, Juan. *The Upanishads*. London: Penguin Books, 1965.

Michelin New England. Michelin Travel Publications, 1993.

Moody, Raymond A. *Reflections on Life After Life*. Covington: Mockingbird Books, 1976.

Narayan, R.K. *The Ramayana: A Shortened Modern Prose Version of the Indian Epic*. New York: Penguin Books, 1977.

O'Neill, Tom. "Onaanraakbaar." *National Geographic*, June 2003, p. 2-31.

Olivelle, Patrick, trans. *Upanishads* (Oxford World's Classics). New York: Oxford University Press, 1998.

Opdebeeck, Anja. *Bijna Dood. Leven met bijna-doodervaringen*. Lannoo, Tielt.

Reisel, M. *Genesis*. Den Haag: Kruseman, 1972.

Ring, Kenneth, and Stephen Franklin. "Do Suicide Survivors Report Near-Death Experiences?" *Omega*, Vol. 12, no. 3, 1981-82, p.191-208.

Ritchie, George G. *Return from Tomorrow*, 33rd ed. Fleming H. Revell (division of Baker Book House Company).

Russell, Bertrand. *A History of Western Philosophy*. New York: Simon and Schuster, 1972.

Schouten, Johan. *Heksenwaan en heksenwaag in oude prenten*. Repro-Holland, Alphen aan den Rijn, 1973.

Shattuck, Cybelle (adapted by Nancy D. Lewis). *The Idiot's Pocket Guide to Hinduism*. Indianapolis: Pearson Education, 2003.

Smith, David. *Hinduism and Modernity*. Oxford (U.K.): Blackwell Publishing, 2003.

Sogyal Rinpoche. *The Tibetan Book of Living and Dying*. London: Ryder (Random House), 2002.

Stokstad, Marilyn. *Art History*. New York: Harry N. Abrams, Inc., 1995.

Storm, Howard. *My Descent into Death: A Second Chance at Life*. New York: Doubleday (Random House), 2005.

Suleman, Azmina. *A Passage to Eternity*. Amethyst Publishing, 2004.

Szulc, Tad. "Abraham: Journey of Faith." *National Geographic*, vol. 200, December, 2001, pp. 90-129.

Taylor, Scott M. *Near-Death Experiences: Discovering and Living in Unity* (dissertation), St. Paul, Minnesota: University of St. Thomas, 2001.

Thurman, A.F. *Het Tibetaans Dodenboek*. Nieuwe vertaling en interpretatie, Uitgeverij Altamira-Becht bv, Bloemendaal, 2000, (original title: *The Tibetan Book of the Dead*. New York: Bantam Books, 1994).

Vanamali, Devi. *The Song of Rama: Visions of the Ramayana*. San Diego, CA.: Blue Dove Press, 2001.

Victoria, Brian Dazen. *Zen War Stories*. London: Routledge Curzon, 2003.

INDEX

About the Author

Christophor Coppes enjoys a career in the international financial sector and currently works at the Dutch Central Bank in Amsterdam monitoring developments in the international financial markets. He holds a PhD in economics from the University of Groningen and has published many scientific articles on finance while maintaining a strong interest in humanitarian issues.

Mr. Coppes's first book was published in 1995 and is based on the true story of how friends and family lovingly looked after a terminally ill AIDSs patient and helped him through the final stages of his life. His second book was written as result of his disgust and horror over the ethnic cleansing that took place under the eyes of Dutch soldiers in Srebrenica during the war in Bosnia Herzegovina in 1995. It was the biggest single massacre in Europe after the Second World War. The story, that really happened, is told from the perspective of one of the victims, a Muslim girl who was a translator for the Dutch United Nation soldiers and one of the Dutch Blue Helmets. His most recent book, *Messages from The Light*, is about the messages that people had during their Near-Death Experiences.

The author lives in Amsterdam. In 2008 he became president of the International Association for Near-Death Studies (IANDS) in the Netherlands. Christophor also demonstrates his social engagement through his work as board member of the Society for Worldwide Dentistry. He has participated in dental projects for underprivileged school children in Kenya, Cambodia, and Nepal.

For more information about Christophor Coppes and further links to websites on Near-Death Experiences please go to www.christophOr.nl.